SACRAMENTO PUBLIC LIBRARY
D0205767
06/12

RABBIT

FAMILY PET GUIDE

The author

David Taylor
BVMS, FRCVS, FZS

David Taylor is a well-known veterinary surgeon, broadcaster and author of over thirty books, including *Small Pet Handbook* (HarperCollins) and six volumes of autobiography, some of which formed the basis for three series of the BBC television drama *One by One*. The founder of the International Zoo Veterinary Group, David has exotic patients across the world, ranging from crocodiles to killer whales and giant pandas. He lives in Richmond, Surrey, with his wife and five Birman cats.

ACKNOWLEDGEMENTS
My super secretaries, Betty and Liz, for typing the manuscript; Heather, my editor, for her skill in transforming sows' ears into silk purses; Louise, for advice and enthusiasm concerning rabbits; my partners in IZVG; Andrew and John, for letting me get on with it; and, of course, my wife, Christine, who persuaded me years ago that rabbits are people and not for eating, ever.

RABBIT

FAMILY PET GUIDE

A PRACTICAL GUIDE TO CARING FOR YOUR RABBIT

DAVID TAYLOR
BVMS, FRCVS, FZS

First published in 1999 by
Collins, an imprint of
HarperCollins*Publishers*
77-85 Fulham Palace Road
Hammersmith, London W6 8JB

www.harpercollins.co.uk

Collins is a registered trademark of
HarperCollins Publishers Limited

This edition published in 2011

15 14 13 12 11
10 9 8 7 6 5 4 3 2 1

© HarperCollins*Publishers*, 1999

David Taylor asserts the moral right to be identified as the author of this work.

All rights reserved. No part of this publication may be reproduced, stored in a retrieval system, or transmitted, in any form or by any means, electronic, mechanical, photocopying, recording or otherwise, without the prior written permission of the publishers.

A catalogue record of this book is available from the British Library.

ISBN 978-0-00-743669-9

This book was created by SP Creative Design for HarperCollinsPublishers
Editor: Heather Thomas
Design and Production: Rolando Ugolini
Photography: David Dalton
Additional photography: Rolando Ugolini: 1, 7, 10, 15, 30 (bottom), 49, 55, 61, 67, 72, 73, 75, 76, 82, 85, 95, 106.

Acknowledgements:
The publishers would like to thank Eileen Early of Brookcroft Bunnery for her kind assistance in producing this book.

Colour reproduction by
Colourscan, Singapore
Printed and bound by
Printing Express Ltd, Hong Kong

Contents

Introduction 6

Origins of the rabbit 8

Varieties of rabbit 18

Behaviour and biology 40

Acquiring a rabbit 56

Housing your rabbit 64

Looking after your rabbit 82

Breeding rabbits 96

Rabbit health 104

First aid 127

Index 128

While every reasonable care was taken in the compilation of this publication, the Publisher and Author cannot accept liability for any loss, damage, injury or death resulting from the keeping of rabbits by user(s) of this publication, or from the use of materials, equipment, methods or information recommended in this publication or from any errors or omissions that may be found in the text of this publication or that may occur at a future date, except as expressly provided by law.

Introduction

Rabbits are on the up and up! Once wrongly regarded as cheap, second-class pets only for children, these delightful and fascinating animals are nowadays third in the league table of species most frequently seen in the vet's waiting room and are favourites among an ever-growing number of adult hobbyists.

It is reckoned that around 1,350,000 rabbits are kept as pets in Britain at the present time and that the United States has a pet rabbit population of over 10,000,000 spread across thirty breeds and about eighty recognised varieties. No longer simply relegated to a cramped wooden hutch in the backyard, the rabbit is to be found in modern, state-of-the-art accommodation with extensive exercising facilities or even indoors as the rather fashionable 'house rabbit' that rubs shoulders, and hogs the hearth-rug, alongside the family cat or dog.

Rabbits are not rodents, nor even closely related to them; they are clean, wholesome creatures to have around, carrying less risk of disease for their human companions than domestic dogs or cats. Gentle and responsive, amenable and cuddly, clever and intelligent, rabbits are ideal pets for folk of all ages. Cheap to run, not needing walks in the park and unlikely to bite the postman or caterwaul on the roof by night, they are easy to keep and maintain.

That said, however, they are like all animals in human care; they demand regular, thoughtful husbandry and proper accommodation. No less intricate in their design than Giant Pandas, no less intriguing in the complexities and sophistication of their physiology than Blue Whales, rabbits deserve, indeed demand, the best of human attention. In return they give us endless pleasure and affection. This book explains how to go about giving the best to, and getting the best from, Brer Rabbit. It is not for the professional breeder or commercial rabbit farmer, but rather the hobbyist and ordinary lover of these marvellous animals.

CHAPTER ONE

Origins of the rabbit

Rabbits and hares — are they furry friends, fiendish pests or providers of food? For thousands of years these small mammals have been closely associated in one way or another with mankind.

Not rodents, but lagomorphs, animals whose name means 'formed like a hare', rabbits occur in the wild in forty-four species spread throughout the world in an amazing variety of habitats. Some, like the Arctic and Snowshoe hares, are creatures of cold Arctic zones. The Antelope hare prefers semi-desert habitats, the Sumatran hare inhabits remote tropical mountain forests, the Swamp rabbit loves paddling about in marshland, whereas the European rabbit can be found in arid deserts, flat grasslands and alpine valleys. Some rabbits and hares are common, whereas others, such as the Yarkand hare of China, the Bushman hare of Africa, the Amami rabbit of Japan and the Volcano rabbit of Mexico, are rare and endangered. Just one specimen of the Sumatran hare has been recorded as seen in the past twenty years.

The only domesticated lagomorph is the rabbit, and all breeds of domesticated rabbit have arisen from the European rabbit (*Oryctolagus cuniculus*) whose original home up to about 2,300 years ago was Spain, some Mediterranean islands and

possibly north-west Africa. The Romans kept domesticated rabbits and, by reintroducing them into their Spanish possessions and crossing them with local wild strains, produced a hardier, more adaptable Spanish rabbit which was eventually imported into northern Europe during the Middle Ages.

Rabbits in Britain

The earliest reference to rabbits in the British Isles is in 1176 in the Scilly Isles. There is evidence of rabbits on the Isle of Wight in the early thirteenth century, where the post of 'rabbit custodian' existed in the manor of Bowcombe. The oldest rabbit remains so far found on the English mainland were in Essex at Rayleigh Castle and date from the late twelfth to early thirteenth centuries. It seems likely that British rabbits were originally imported by the Normans at the time of the Conquest in 1066.

However, some zoologists believe that rabbits may have reached Britain before the Normans. Fossilized remains record their presence before the third Glacial Age (22,000 years ago). It is certain that they did not survive the icy conditions. Perhaps, after the ice receded, Europe and North Africa were repopulated with rabbits moving out from the Iberian Peninsula. Rabbits may then have crossed the land bridge between France and

Left: *The modern domesticated rabbit has its origins in Spain.*

Britain around 7000–6000BC; England was connected to the Continent up to about 5000BC. It is also possible that the Romans, enthusiastic trenchermen who had domesticated rabbits by the first century BC, may have introduced some of these animals.

Did you know?

In 1387, William of Wykeham forbade his nuns from bringing to church 'birds, hounds, rabbits or other frivolous things that promote indiscipline'. Apparently the ladies of the convents kept pet rabbits even in those days.

Food and predators

By mediaeval times, rabbits were much valued for their meat, skin and fur. Rabbit foetuses taken from killed does were considered 'meatless' and thus a permissible food on fast days. A fine buck rabbit fetched as high a price as a suckling pig.

Later, with the development of agriculture and a decline in the numbers of natural predators,

Right: *Originally a valuable food animal, the rabbit took centuries to become a popular pet.*

such as falcons and wild carnivores, rabbits became more of a problem for the farmer. Hunting, trapping, snaring and ferreting kept the numbers down to some degree, and rabbits remained in demand for food and the fur trade. However, three rabbits can eat as much vegetable food as one sheep in a day and so by the nineteenth century the loss of arable produce was significant. The rabbit had become an important pest.

Among the more bizarre methods used in attempting to rid fields of rabbits was that of farmers in the Isle of Wight. They fixed lighted candles to the backs of crabs and sent them down rabbit burrows, presumably to frighten the rabbits into moving out!

Germ warfare, the deliberate spreading of a viral rabbit disease, was a more modern experiment in controlling rabbits — and one that, in some places, went disastrously wrong. But more of that later (see page 123).

The spread of the European rabbit

Rabbits were first introduced into South Africa by the governor of the now infamous Robben Island in April 1654 as a source of meat for vessels going to the Orient.

Australia's first rabbits, probably domestic Silver Greys, arrived at Botany Bay, New South Wales, with the British First Fleet carrying the early English colonists in 1788. New Zealand likewise had rabbits introduced by early settlers who obtained stock from Australia.

Although the United States possesses indigenous species of rabbits and hares (Jackrabbits, Snowshoe hares, Cottontail rabbits, Brush rabbits, etc.), the European rabbit arrived only relatively recently.

At the turn of the century, rabbits were

Did you know?

The rabbit is not mentioned in the Bible. The biblical 'coney', often mistakenly referred to as a rabbit, is in fact the Syrian hyrax, a small marmot-like mammal whose closest living relative is the elephant.

plentiful on the San Juan islands off the Washington coast. A lighthouse keeper on Smith Island at the mouth of Puget Sound had imported domesticated varieties (Belgian Hares and Black Flemish rabbits) in order to sell their pelts and meat in Seattle. His successor released them and they multiplied rapidly as is their fashion!

Later, rabbits were introduced from San Juan to Ohio, Pennsylvania, Indiana, New Jersey, Wisconsin and Maryland. Luckily for the agriculture of these states, none of the introductions were successful.

Having spoken of the spread of the European rabbit and its domesticated descendants across the world, it is worth adding that there has been also a movement of some New World wild rabbits into Europe in recent years. In the 1960s, the American eastern Cottontail rabbit, which is resistant to myxomatosis, was introduced for sporting purposes into northern Italy and, later, to France and northern Spain. In the early 1980s, New England Cottontails were introduced into Germany.

Did you know?

Rabbits tend to crop up frequently in historical slang; a 'rabbit skin' was an academical hood in the last century, a 'rabbit sucker' was a spendthrift or pawnbroker, and a 'rabbit-pie shifter' was a nickname for a policeman.

Right: *The Silver is one of the oldest breeds and may, according to some experts, have its roots in India or even Thailand.*

Wild rabbits of the world

Lagomorphs, a zoological order that includes rabbits, hares and pikas (small creatures up to about 25 cm/10 in long with rounded ears, short legs and virtually no tail which live in mountainous regions of Russia and the Himalayas) have been around for some 55,000,000 years after originating in northern Asia. The European rabbit was the first and only lagomorph to be domesticated around 3,000 years ago, whereas the modern pet rabbit in all its sizes, shapes, colours and coat patterns is essentially a product of the past 130 years only. This is quite unlike the pet dog, the history of whose breeds goes back in some cases for many centuries.

Most of us are familiar with the common species of wild rabbits in our home countries, but we may forget what a rich variety of rabbits and hares exists on this planet. Bunny is anything but boring, often mysterious and sometimes very rare.

As mentioned earlier, rabbits and hares are extremely versatile animals. They can be found in a broad spectrum of

Did you know?

The rapid spread of rabbits across Australia was greatly helped by the existence of 'ready-made homes'— burrows left behind by wombats, boodies and greater bilbies, all tunnel-digging marsupials.

Wild European rabbits

Apart from San Juan, the only other stocks of wild — feral, meaning gone back to the wild, would perhaps be a better word — European rabbits at present in the United States are on South Farallon Island, west of San Francisco, Santa Barbara, the Anacapa Islands in the Pacific off the coast of Los Angeles, Middleton Island in the Gulf of Alaska and on Manana, Lehua and Molokini islands in Hawaii.

habitats, some species preferring a cold climate, whereas others thrive in hot deserts, on river banks or in humid forests. Some, like the Hispid hare or Assam rabbit, have coarse, bristly coats, while others, such as the Red Rock hare, sport coats that are thick and woolly. Coat colours of hairs and rabbits can be grey, dark brown, buff or red, and while some lack much in the way of markings, others, such as the Sumatran hare, have distinctive dark stripes. There are rabbits and hares (for example, the Arctic hare and Pygmy rabbit) that dig burrows, and others (Cottontail rabbits and European hares) that do not, and either nest above ground or prefer to occupy burrows made by other animals.

Domestication

So how did it come to pass that the domesticated pet or fancy rabbit came on to the scene? Firstly, the Romans found that by taking litters of young wild rabbits, they could rear them for the pot. The rabbits were kept in special walled enclosures called *leporaria*. Later, in Europe during the Dark Ages, noblemen and monasteries continued this primitive form of 'rabbit farming'. Over a period of time, by a process of spontaneous mutation and natural selection, varieties of size and coat colour arose. Again by natural selection, more tractable wild does

Right: *The short-haired Rex originated in France in 1919.*

CHAPTER
ONE

would thrive and breed better in captivity and pass on their tractability to their offspring. Gradually, over many years, a tamer, 'domesticated' kind of rabbit emerged — still the same species as its wild relative but much easier to handle.

Artificial selection — the process by which human beings select and breed certain rabbits that have desirable qualities — also occurred over the centuries. Some characteristics were encouraged for purely commercial reasons: bigger animals that would yield more meat; individuals with fur that was better in some way for the furrier and perhaps coloured; and does that were more prolific breeders. It was not until the nineteenth century, however, that artificial selection for purely cosmetic reasons arose. Size, body shape, colour and coat pattern became the interest of the rabbit fancier, in contrast to the rabbit farmer, and controlled breeding gave rise to the rich range of rabbit breeds that we have today.

Below: *The duo-colour French Lop has, like many breeds, evolved through selective breeding.*

Although the rabbit fancier and the rabbit farmer are poles apart in their objectives and methods, there has been some cross-fertilization of ideas (as well as of bucks and does!) during the increase in numbers and breeds over the past 150 years. In 1850, there were ten breeds of rabbits in Great Britain. However, in 1995, the total number of breeds was sixty-one with 531 varieties. Worldwide there are over 200 rabbit breeds with innumerable varieties.

Did you know?

There are more breeds of rabbit than of any other domesticated mammal except the dog.

All domestic rabbits are of the same single species — *Oryctolagus cuniculus*. The term 'breed' refers to a group of animals whose physical characteristics resemble those of one another more than they do those of another breed. The term 'variety' refers to the rabbit's coat colour.

Up to about 1850, domestic rabbits comprised some of pure coat colour, Silvers, Lops with bigger bodies and long ears, and the majority, which were spotted or patterned. The Rex is a mutation first found in France in 1919; a later mutation of the Rex occurred in the United States to produce the Satin.

Breed standards today

Nowadays, international breed standards are laid down by governing bodies of the rabbit fancy in many countries. In Britain, domestic rabbits are divided into two groups:

- The fancy breeds
- The fur breeds

The fur breeds are divided into normal fur breeds (breeds with coats composed of an undercoat with longer guard hairs), Rex breeds (breeds with guard hairs shorter than the undercoat) and Satin breeds (breeds with special, shiny coat hairs).

CHAPTER TWO

Varieties of rabbit

Today's rabbit has come a long way since its origins thousands of years ago. These are now many varieties of rabbit in different sizes and coat colours, including normal fur, fancy, rex and satin breeds.

What exactly is a rabbit? We have said that it is a lagomorph, not a rodent, and, like all lagomorphs, which also include the hares and pikas, it shares certain common characteristics — long, soft fur, furry feet (unlike most rodents), large ears, and eyes that are set high and on the sides of the head. The nose has split-shaped nostrils which 'wink' open and closed, and the rabbit's neck, although short and feeble, can turn to a greater extent than those of rodents. Let's look at some of these wonderful breeds more closely.

Origins of the name

The names for 'rabbit' (which is an exception and may derive from the Walloon word 'rabett') in central European languages all stem from the Latin *cuniculus*: German *kaninchen*, Spanish *conejo*, Portuguese *coclho*, Italian *coniglio*, Old French *connin*, Danish and Swedish *kaning*, Belgian *konin*, Welsh *cuningen* and old English *conyng* and *coney*.

CHAPTER TWO

Rabbit breeds

NORMAL FUR BREEDS

- [ ] Alaska
- [ ] American
- [ ] Argente
- [ ] Beaver (now extinct)
- [ ] Beige (now extinct)
- [ ] Beveren
- [ ] Blanc de Bonscat (rare)
- [ ] Blanc de Hotot
- [ ] Blanc de Termonde
- [ ] Blue Imperial
- [ ] Brabancon (now extinct)
- [ ] British Giant
- [ ] Californian
- [ ] Chifox
- [ ] Chinchilla
- [ ] Chinchilla Giganta
- [ ] Deilenaar (rare)
- [ ] Florida White
- [ ] Fox
- [ ] Glavcot
- [ ] Havana
- [ ] Isabella (rare)
- [ ] Lilac
- [ ] New Zealand
- [ ] Nubian (now extinct)
- [ ] Perle de Hal
- [ ] Perlfee
- [ ] Pointed Beveren
- [ ] Sable
- [ ] Sallander
- [ ] Siberian
- [ ] Sitka (now extinct)
- [ ] Smoke Pearl
- [ ] Squirrel
- [ ] Sussex
- [ ] Swiss Fox
- [ ] Theringes
- [ ] Vienna Blue

❖ *Lynx Rex*

FANCY BREEDS

- [ ] Angora
- [ ] Belgian Hare
- [ ] Dutch
- [ ] English
- [ ] Flemish Giant
- [ ] Giant Papillon
- [ ] Harlequin
- [ ] Himalayan
- [ ] Lop
- [ ] Lotharinger
- [ ] Netherland Dwarf
- [ ] Palomino
- [ ] Polish
- [ ] Rhinelander (rare)
- [ ] Silver
- [ ] Tan
- [ ] Thrianta

REX BREEDS

- [ ] Agouti Rex
- [ ] Miniature Rex
- [ ] Rough Coated Rex
- [ ] Satin Rex
- [ ] Self Rex
- [ ] Shaded Rex

SATIN BREEDS

- [ ] Argente
- [ ] Beige
- [ ] Black
- [ ] Blue
- [ ] Bronze
- [ ] Brown
- [ ] Castor
- [ ] Chinchilla
- [ ] Cinnamon
- [ ] Fawn
- [ ] Fox
- [ ] Havana
- [ ] Himalayan
- [ ] Ivory
- [ ] Lilac
- [ ] Lynx
- [ ] Marten Sable
- [ ] Opal
- [ ] Orange
- [ ] Seal Point
- [ ] Siamese Sable
- [ ] Smoke Pearl
- [ ] Sooty Fawn
- [ ] Squirrel

CHAPTER
TWO

NORMAL FUR BREEDS

Alaska

■ ***Appearance:*** An elegant rabbit with a sleek, silky black coat.
■ ***Breed history:*** The Alaska may have arisen in the 1920s in France from melanistic forms of the Himalayan rabbit.

American

■ ***Appearance:*** This large breed has white fur and pink eyes or blue fur and eyes.
■ ***Notes:*** Not often seen outside the United States.

Argente

■ ***Appearance:*** The Argente's coat is silvery over an undercoat of grey-blue. Other varieties are the Bleu, Crème and Brun.
■ ***Breed history:*** Another old breed, indeed the Argente Champagne is the oldest of the fur breeds and is known to have existed in France in the seventeenth century. It may have originated in Indo-China but is more likely to be a descendant of the Silver Grey. The latter's name derives not from its coat colour, but from the region of France where it has been popular for at least 300 years.

❖ *Argente Brun*

Beveren

■ ***Appearance:*** The Beveren has a gorgeous, full, silky fur

and comes in five colours: blue, white, black, brown and lilac.
■ ***Breed history:*** A late nineteenth-century development from Belgium.

Blanc de Hotot

■ ***Appearance:*** A shiny white coloured rabbit with brown eyes surrounded by 4–7-cm/1½–3-in wide black rings.
■ ***Breed history:*** This striking breed was created in France and is still very popular there.

British Giant

■ ***Appearance:*** It is essentially the same as the Flemish Giant but, unlike the latter which comes only in a steely-grey colour, the British Giant can be white, black, blue, dark steel grey or brownish grey. Truly a giant, it grows to weigh over 5.5 kg/12 lb.
■ ***Breed history:*** It was developed in the 1940s from coloured strains of Flemish Giant in the United States.

❖ British Giant Agouti

Californian

❖ Californian

■ ***Appearance:*** Mainly white with black tips to feet and ears.
■ ***Breed history:*** A very pretty rabbit, this is a true American. It was produced in the United States in the 1920s for commercial purposes from crosses of New Zealand White, Himalayan and Chinchilla rabbits.

Chinchilla

Appearance: The Chinchilla's coat resembles that of the real Chinchilla, an unrelated rodent from the South American Andes mountain range.

Breed history: A mutant developed before World War I in France, this breed is a popular exhibition animal. It first arrived in the United States in 1919. Two related breeds are the American Chinchilla and the American Giant Chinchilla.

❖ *Chinchilla*

❖ *Chinchilla Rex*

Florida White

Breed history: Not normally a pet rabbit, this attractive little rabbit from the American Florida Keys was, sadly, developed for the laboratory and meat industries.

Cross-breeding

Attempts have been made to cross the European rabbit with some species of its nearest relative, the Cottontail rabbit. However, although fertilization has taken place, no live births have been recorded.

New Zealand Red

Appearance: The New Zealand may have red, white or even 'blue' fur. The New Zealand Red has a rich ochre-coloured but rather coarse fur.

Breed history: Not an antipodean but rather an American rabbit originally, the New Zealand Red was developed from Flemish Giants and Belgian Hares.

Perlfee

Appearance: The Perlfee is small (about 2.5 kg/5½ lb) and lilac-grey in colour.

Breed history: A rarely seen German rabbit. It is descended from the Havana.

Variations

Many breeds of rabbit come in a variety of colours and sub-types, i.e. Dwarf and Rex. For example, the New Zealand rabbit may be blue or white, as shown here, as well as red.

Top right: New Zealand Blue Right: New Zealand White

CHAPTER
TWO

Sable

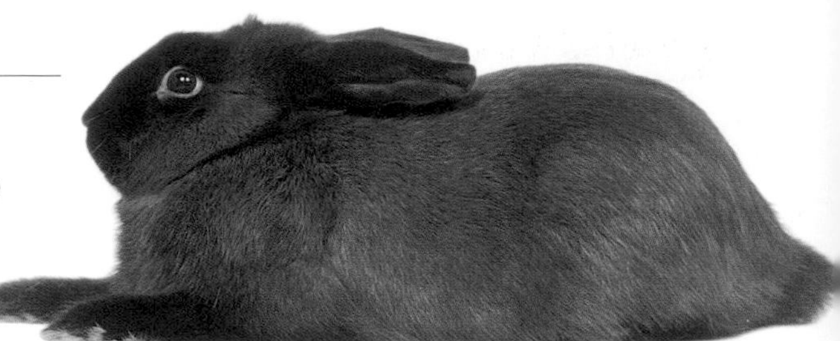

Sable Siamese Medium

Appearance: These handsome rabbits with magnificent coats come in two varieties: Siamese and Marten.

Breed history: In both varieties, the basic coat colour originally resembled that of the north Asian member of the weasel family called the Sable. Similarly, the Siamese and Marten are so named because they do look a little like the Siamese cat and the Stone or Beech marten of Europe and Central Asia.

Sallander

Sallander

Appearance: It is a very pretty animal with a dense pearl-white coat that possesses long, café-au-lait guard hairs giving it an overall smoky effect. The lower half of the body is coffee shaded.

Breed history: Yet another rabbit of the Netherlands, the Sallander was originally developed from the Thuringer.

Sussex

Appearance: The original type was the Sussex Gold with a rich red-gold coat, shaded in light brown or lilac. Later came the Sussex Cream — rich cream with delicate light lilac ticking.

Breed history: This is a recent product (1986) of crossing Californian and Lilac rabbits.

Swiss Fox

Appearance: Medium-sized and stocky with almost no neck, the Swiss Fox has a fairly long coat and comes in white and several colours.

Breed history: This breed arose in both Switzerland and Germany in the 1920s.

Swiss Fox

Vienna Blue

Appearance: The Vienna Blue has a magnificent blue coat. Other varieties are white, black, brown, grey and blue-grey.

Breed history: Here is a most popular breed of middle-sized rabbit. It is quite big (3.5–5.5 kg/7½–12 lb), being descended from crosses of continental Giant breeds with the injection of Argente blood.

Did you know?

The Roman polymath, Pliny the Elder, wrote in the first century AD of how, at the time of Christ, rabbits had devastated the countryside on the island of Majorca. The people living there begged Emperor Augustus for military assistance in combating the animals or alternatively would he please find them somewhere else to live. The Imperial legions must have been sent, one assumes, for that popular tourist destination is nowadays far from overrun by bunnies.

CHAPTER
TWO

FANCY BREEDS

Angora

Appearance: Most Angoras are white albinos but they come in a dozen other colours, too.

Breed history: An old breed, once known as the English Silkhaired Rabbit, the Angora was certainly around in the early eighteenth century. It is the only breed whose fur can be spun into wool. Like long-haired cats, its fur must be groomed regularly to prevent the formation of troublesome 'cots'.

Blue and Gold Angoras

Belgian Hare

Appearance: Rather hare-like with a rich red-brown agouti coat.

Breed history: Although originating in Belgium, this breed was developed and refined in Britain after arriving there in the late 1800s. At about the same time, it was exported also to the United States. It may share a now-extinct ancestor, the Patagonian, with the very different-looking Flemish Giant. The first Belgian Hare club was formed in England in 1887.

Dwarf

❖ *Dwarf Lop Magpie Blue*

Appearance: The so-called dwarf factor is responsible for the round heads, big eyes, short ears and plump little bodies typical of these very popular creatures although some recent dwarf breeds (e.g. the Mini-lop) have been produced without the dwarf features and should perhaps be considered as small versions of standard Lops rather than true dwarves.

Breed history: There are many breeds of Dwarf rabbit besides the Netherlands dwarf. Basically mini-versions of the larger breeds, they were first developed from the Polish rabbit in the nineteenth century as Ermine dwarves. In the twentieth century, the genetic basis for rabbit dwarfism was pinpointed by breeders in America.

❖ *Dwarf Lop*

Dutch

Appearance: It comes in eight bicoloured varieties and also a tricoloured one. This fairly small rabbit is renowned for acting, when needed, as a first-class foster mother.

Breed history: Like so many people, my first pet rabbit as a boy was a Dutch. The breed did indeed arise in the Lowlands from where it was first imported into England at the beginning of the nineteenth century.

Dutch Black and White

English

Appearance: Delightfully patterned and usually with a face decorated with a coloured butterfly 'smut', it comes in five colours.

Breed history: The English is a very old breed.

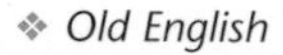

Old English

Flemish Giant

Appearance: A heavyweight among fancy rabbits, a Flemish Giant can tip the scales at almost 10 kg/22 lb.

Notes: Fully extended, the toe tip to toe tip length can approach 95 cm/38 in. One male, 'Floppy', tipped the scales at 11.03 kg/24 lb at his death, aged eight. In Britain, the only colour officially recognised is steely grey. The Flemish Giant does have a small dewlap on the throat.

Did you know?

Puffins on Puffin Island, off Anglesey in north Wales regularly evict rabbits from their burrows during the birds' nesting season, muscling in and 'squatting' in the holes until their chicks are reared!

Giant Papillon

Appearance: France's answer to the English; the markings of this rabbit are similar although the flanks usually sport patches rather than spots.

❖ *Papillon*

Harlequin

Appearance: Available in eight colour varieties, the one in which the chequered red gold or fawn is replaced by fawn is called a Magpie.

Breed history: Known in some countries as the Japanese, this attractive breed was developed in France at the end of the nineteenth century from Tortoiseshell Dutch rabbits.

Harlequin Blue

Harlequin Black

Himalayan

Appearance: The Himalayan is basically an albino with coloured tips to the body.

Breed history: A friendly amenable rabbit, the Himalayan has no connections with the mountains. It is known in some countries as the Russian or Chinese and may have originated in the Far East. The coloured tips to its body are pigmentation that arises during early life when the cooler surface temperatures of the extremities stimulate the invasion and multiplication of pigment-carrying cells.

Some breeders have tried to accelerate this process by frequently bathing young rabbits' feet, ears and muzzle in cold water. Although not cruel, I do not recommend this practice.

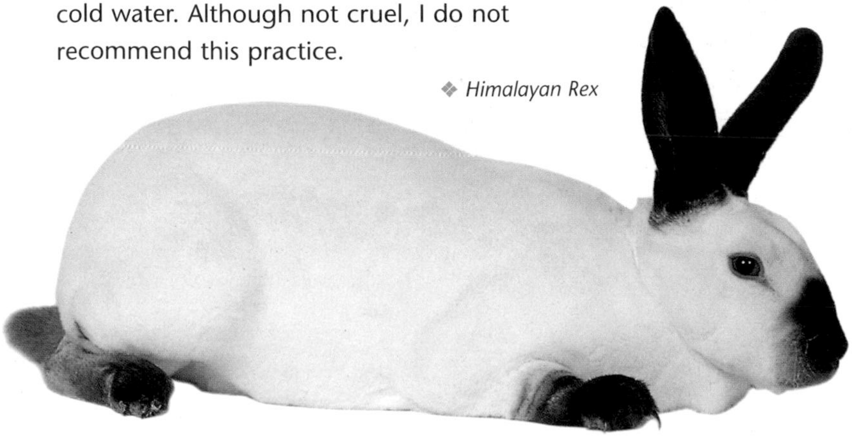

❖ *Himalayan Rex*

Lotharinger

■ ***Appearance:*** Built like a Flemish Giant and with markings resembling the Rhinelander, this breed is basically white with broad black eye rings and black butterfly patching of the nostrils. There is a black spot beneath each eye and five to eight black spots on the haunches and flanks. The ears, neck and spine are also black.

Did you know?

Brer Rabbit, the literary creation immortalized by Joel Chandler Harris, is usually depicted as a Cottontail rabbit. However, he was probably a hare, since black slaves brought to the United States from Africa carried their legends with them, and the hare rather than the rabbit is ubiquitous in African folklore as the most sharp-witted of animals.

Lops

❖ *Cashmere Lop Seal Point*

■ ***Appearance:*** These striking long-eared rabbits all originated from the old English Lop.

■ ***Breed history:*** The English Lop, the first breed ever to be exhibited, was crossed with European Giant breeds to create the French Lop from which, in turn, came the German Lop and Dwarf Lop. Later developments from the Dwarf Lop include the Cashmere Lop and the Miniature Lop. Whereas a typical French Lop will weigh approximately 5.5 kg/12 lb, Miniature Lops should not exceed 1.6 kg/3½ lb.

❖ *German White Lop*

❖ *English Lop*

Netherlands Dwarf

■ ***Appearance:*** This sweet, little (just over 1 kg/2 lb) rabbit is available in various colours.

❖ *Netherlands Dwarf White*

❖ *Netherlands Dwarf Siamese Sable Dark*

■ ***Breed history:*** The Netherlands Dwarf was created in Holland from the Polish rabbit at the turn of the century.

■ ***Notes:*** Makes a perfect children's pet.

❖ *Netherlands Fawn Dwarf*

What's in a name?

In days gone by, country folk gave quaint names to various sorts of wild rabbit.

- 'Warreners' lived in established warrens.
- 'Parkers' were rabbits of open country.
- 'Hedgehogs' were those of thickly wooded areas or, alternatively, 'of no fixed abode'!
- 'Sweethearts' were rabbits bred in captivity. Sweethearts of the eighteenth and nineteenth centuries were normally kept in pits and fed on brewery grains, cabbage leaves, turnip tops and other vegetable refuse.

Palomino

Appearance: Another much-acclaimed American rabbit that comes in either lynx or golden colours. The lynx is blazing orange in colour with a white undercoat, whereas the golden has a lush, light gold coat with a white or cream undercoat.

Polish

Appearance: This is an elegant, petite character weighing 1.5–2 kg/3–4 lb. It can be found in a wide range of varieties.

Far left: Polish Siamese Sable.
Left: Polish Martin Smoke

Rhinelander

Appearance: A tricoloured rabbit.

Breed history: From Germany, the Rhinelander is a product of English and Harlequin crosses. It is not a common breed.

Silver

Appearance: The Silver Grey's coat is black with white ticking, which produces the 'silver' effect. Other colours are brown, blue and fawn. Baby Silvers do not have the characteristic ticking; it appears gradually after their first moult.

Breed history: A most ancient breed that was certainly around in the early seventeenth century, the first of the Silvers was undoubtedly the Silver Grey.

Notes: Silvers are a hardy breed and excellent both as show animals and as children's pets.

Silver

Tan

Appearance: Originally Tans were black, but crossings with sooty fawn rabbits produced blues. Now they can be found also in chocolate and lilac. All Tans have a characteristic coat pattern with a back of one particular colour, lighter coloured underparts and buff flanks, ears, feet and nostrils.

Breed history: Tans originated from interbreeding between wild and domesticated rabbits in the late nineteenth century.

Thrianta

Appearance: The Thrianta has glorious red-orange fur.

Breed history: Not very often seen, this Dutch breed of rabbit is of fairly recent origin.

CHAPTER TWO

SATIN BREEDS

Satins

Appearance: These rabbits have distinctive coats displaying a satin-like sheen. This is due to a mutation that altered the usual structure of the guard hairs of the rabbit's fur.

Ivory satin

Breed history: Developed in the 1930s in the United States, they were originally albinos (Ivory Satins) but nowadays there are also many colour varieties as well as Satin Rexes whose coats combine Satin sheen with the typical Rex form of fur.

Havana

Appearance: It has lush chocolate-brown fur.

Breed history: This is another rabbit that originated in the Netherlands. The Havana was first developed in a village called Ingen and was nicknamed the Ingen Fire-eye because of its eyes which glow bright red in dim light.

Lilac

Appearance: This breed possesses fine oyster-coloured fur.

Breed history: First appearing on the scene in 1910, the Lilac was produced by breeding Blue Beverens with Havanas and then interbreeding their progeny. Similar rabbits were bred in Holland and Germany and called the Gouda or Gouwenaar and the Marburger respectively. The Lilac has a very placid nature.

REX BREEDS

Rex

❖ Rex Tortoiseshell

■ ***Appearance:*** The peculiar arrangement of the hairs of the coat with the guard hairs shorter than the undercoat is the characteristic of the Rex. It produces a lustrous, velvety effect which was highly prized by furriers. The Rexes can be found in a broad spectrum of colours and also patterns.

■ ***Breed history:*** There are four types of Rex: the smooth-coated Standard; the rare Astrex with tightly waved fur; the Mini Rex, a mini-version of the Standard Rex weighing around 1.5 kg/3 lb; and the Opossum Rex, also rare and with a silvery coat.

❖ *Rex Dalmatian*

❖ *Magpie Rex*

❖ *Otter Rex*

CHAPTER THREE

Behaviour and biology

The words 'dumb bunny' may apply to certain homo sapiens *of a rather scatty nature, but definitely not to our friend the rabbit. Many scientists consider rabbits to be more intelligent than pigeons, and at least one researcher has done experiments which claim to show that dolphins are no more intelligent than pigeons, so let's shout about rabbits being sharper than dolphins!*

Pet rabbit behaviour

I will talk later on about rabbit vocal and foot drumming communications (see page 51), but rabbits can express their feelings, desires and prejudices in several other ways. Having a rabbit as a pet is to enjoy a loving relationship with an interactive friend which is quite different and much more rewarding than having a tank full of guppies or a tortoise in the garden.

Some aspects of rabbit behaviour have already been mentioned, but let's look at a few more examples of bunny body language.

Did you know?

A pub in Bristol employed an aggressive, indeed rather violent, rabbit called Loopylugs as a 'guard-dog'. His son Loopylugs Junior took over after Loopylugs Senior was killed by intruders.

CHAPTER THREE

Body language

■ Gently nudging you with its nose: this may mean 'hello' or it may often indicate a wish to be petted.

■ Licking your hand: an expression of affection, as in cats, or a gesture of thanks for some small favour.

■ Pushing your hand away: 'That's enough stroking, thank you.'

■ Lying flat on its stomach with ears folded back close to the body, and eyes open and alert: this usually means the rabbit is preparing for trouble — apprehension.

■ As above but with eyes half-closed: 'I'd like a nap now if you don't mind.'

■ Sitting on its haunches: 'Let's see, hear and smell what's going on.'

■ Rolling on the ground: 'I feel great!'

■ Squatting with ears folded back: content with life.

■ Rising up and jumping on hind legs: this indicates happy excitement and curiosity.

■ Tense body with head and ears stretched forwards and

Did you know?

Rabbits normally live for six to eight years, but there are records of them living eighteen years!

Above: *Licking your hand is an expression of affection.*

Left: *This house rabbit is sitting on its haunches content with life.*

straight tail-bob: intense concentration tinged with caution.

■ Snuggling up to you or following you around the house or garden honking softly: 'I really love you.'

■ Shaking the ears briefly: mild annoyance (but check that there is no irritation due to ear disease).

■ Lying on side with both hind legs extended: tired or hot.

■ Tense upright stance with tail extended as much as possible and ears laid back: 'I'm going to attack.'

■ Scratching the floor: attention-seeking or attempting to make a burrow (often seen in does in oestrus or pregnant, and in bucks becoming agitated when rivals are around).

■ Nipping with the teeth: between rabbits it usually means 'Move over please.' Nipping you means 'I've had enough of that!'

Right: *This rabbit is relaxing on the sofa after another hard day in the run.*

CHAPTER THREE

The senses

Eyes

The sight of rabbits is excellent; with the eyes set well out on both sides of the head, they can cover a field of over 300 degrees. Great flexibility of the neck further assists to provide virtually all-round vision. The eyes can move either in conjunction, or separately, but because of their lateral positioning with no overlapping of the visual fields, they cannot see stereoscopically like human beings, monkeys or cats. However, whereas stereoscopic ability to judge distances precisely is important to predators, such as cats, by and large it is not that vital in prey animals, such as rabbits, where all-round vision is more of a life-saver!

Other creatures that usually find themselves playing the part of innocent victims, e.g. the mouse, shrew and partridge, also have eyes set to the sides like the rabbit. The problem is the area in front of the nose, particularly the nearest 2 m/6 ft, which is poorly seen by the rabbit or hare. To overcome this difficulty, it has to tip its head a little to one side so that one eye at a time can scan the awkward zone.

The position of the eyes explains why, when a hare is pursued by a dog, it lifts its head up and

Right: *Rabbits have an excellent field of vision but cannot see stereoscopically like human beings.*

Above: *The red colour of an albino's eyes is caused by a layer of blood vessels behind the retina.*

lays its ears back. It can see the dog behind but it has that blind spot dead ahead and in full flight there's no time to mess about tipping its head to right or left. Consequently, hares sometimes dash headlong over a cliff or straight into a pair of human legs!

There is no shimmering, reflecting mirror behind the retina of a rabbit as seen in a hunter, such as the cat. The red colour of an albino's eyes is simply the layer of blood vessels behind the retina. There is also, however, an intriguing dull eyeshine frequently seen in rabbits; scientists do not understand how this is produced. The retina, the light-sensitive 'film' of the eye, is much more highly organised and complex in rabbits than in man or other primates. Whereas the rabbit sorts out and interprets in the retina itself

Did you know?

An attacking snake cannot hypnotise a rabbit before striking; the rabbit 'freezes' instinctively as it knows that the snake cannot distinguish an immobile animal from a lifeless object. When rabbits 'freeze' in the glare of oncoming car headlights, however, things don't always go so well.

much of the visual information coming into the eye, higher creatures, such as primates, have shifted such functions back into the more sophisticated sight-control areas of the brain.

Ears and hearing

The large size and mobility of the rabbit's ears indicate that hearing is probably the animal's most important sense. Swivelling quickly, these highly sensitive 'dishes' can collect the faintest of sounds from the air.

Smell

Smell is another sense that is very important to rabbits, both for their gourmet food-hunting and their social lives. They are most competent sniffers. When they are 'winking' their nose in typical fashion, you can glimpse an oval pad set on the septum that separates the left and right nostrils. This pad contains microscopic sense organs which may be involved with smelling at a distance, and possibly some other information-extracting function that we don't yet understand. The winking alternately covers and exposes the pad as if the air is being tested for any chemical molecules it might be carrying.

Rabbits have scent glands within the chin and at the anus. Bucks use odours to mark out territory and possessions (including

Marking territory

Wild and domesticated rabbits are often seen scratching their chins with their hind legs which are then stamped on the ground. No, they haven't got an itch or skin disease. What they are doing is transferring a scent produced by glands in the skin of the chin. By this means they mark the boundaries of their territory.

Left and below: *This rabbit is pricking its ears to catch the faintest of sounds which may warn of danger. Hearing is the rabbits most important and highly developed sense. The large ear 'flaps' act like television or radar dishes, collecting sound waves rather than electronic signals.*

Left: *Note how the rabbit raises its body and swivels round its ear flaps to improve sound reception.*

A keen hunter by smell

Rabbits are such accomplished sniffers that they can go hunting (like pigs and trained dogs) for the elusive and sought after underground truffle fungus by scent alone. However, they are by no means smelly creatures with little body scent — just as well in a world full of keen-nosed predators such as foxes. A fox, which can locate eggs buried 10 cm/4 in deep when passing by at a distance of 2.7 m/8½ ft, normally misses baby rabbits buried in sand by their mother when she goes out searching for food.

chosen females and young belonging to them) either by rubbing their chins against objects and then transferring the scent from their chins onto their paws and then stamping it along their boundary lines, or by spraying urine in the manner of tom cats, often with considerable accuracy and range. Chin-scratching in rabbits thus denotes male chauvinism rather than a troublesome itch or a moment of puzzlement!

The anal scent glands secrete odours which are attached to the droppings rather like chemical calling cards. By sniffing these

Right: *Rabbits have a very keen sense of smell.*

Above: *Rabbits are often fussy eaters with a better sense of taste than humans.*

snippets of information, rabbits can recognise one another, deduce the sex and age of another individual, where it has been and much more.

Wild rabbits mark the entrances to their burrows, rocks and bushes, and pet rabbits do the same to their hutch, nest box, chair, etc. Dominant bucks and does do more marking than submissive ones, and no rabbit feels happy in strange territory that is either unmarked or marked by a 'foreign' rabbit.

Dominant, rather aggressive rabbits possess larger scent glands and secrete more complex odours than subordinate ones. The smells produced by the two types of rabbit are so different that even human nostrils can distinguish them.

Taste

With such a cornucopia of flavours to be found in the plant world, it is not surprising to find that rabbits also have a highly developed

sense of taste. Oh, the delight of comparing a mouthful of hogweed here with a stem or two of sow thistle there, and maybe some coltsfoot as a dessert! The mouth of the rabbit epicure possesses 17,000 taste buds compared to 10,000 in the human, a mere 400 in parrots and a niggardly 30–60 in pigeons.

Touch

Although the rabbit's entire body surface has receptors in the skin which receive tactile stimuli, the long whiskers (usually about as long as the body is wide) are especially important touch-antennae, particularly at night. The whiskers also feel for the walls of the familiar dark tunnels under the ground, and the contours of the home burrow are registered in the kinaesthetic (touch) memory areas of the brain. Put a rabbit in a strange burrow and the alarm bells begin ringing in this programmed memory bank; under such conditions, a rabbit is apt to panic. So unpleasant is the idea of a

Below: *Smaller rabbits are more efficient users of food than the large breeds such as the Blue Angora pictured here.*

foreign burrow to a rabbit that it would rather seek any other sort of refuge (bushes, long grass, etc.), even with a hunter hot on its heels, than use a handy hole belonging to somebody else!

Weight

Lagomorphs range in weight from 100 g/3½ oz for the smallest pikas up to around 4.6 kg/10 lb for the largest wild hares. However domestic breeds of rabbit can exceed that with weights of 5.5–6.3 kg/12 –13¾ lb, generally in adult Flemish Giants; the record is 11.3 kg/25 lb, which was achieved by a Flemish Giant. It must be admitted, however, that rabbits are not particularly efficient users of food. The rate at which they extract available energy from foodstuffs is only about one-third of that achieved by sheep or cows. However, they are more 'damp-resistant' than sheep, and they have survived in wet, chilly environments that have wiped out sheep flocks.

Did you know?

A rather bellicose rabbit named Harvey who had been the victim of mistreatment was adopted by the American Society for the Prevention of Cruelty to Animals and became the focal point for a campaign against animal abuse in the late 1970s. He bit sixteen people during his lifetime.

Voice

Some rabbits do give little grunts of pleasure and they may make other sounds, some of which are not easily heard by the human ear, in certain circumstances. For example, rabbits may emit a loud piercing scream when in great pain or caught by a predator or hunter; bucks in breeding condition may purr; rabbits may growl when aggressive; utter a very low squeal or whimper when tired of being handled or played with; grind their teeth for no apparent reason, or, if loud and the animal is depressed, as a sign of pain; hiss when about to attack; and mutter when annoyed. Another non-vocal noise made by rabbits is drumming of the hind feet on the floor. This is a sign of being afraid, and in wild rabbits it is a warning of danger for their companions.

CHAPTER
THREE

Did you know?

'I am at a loss to know whether it be my hare's foot which is my preservative, or my taking of a pill of turpentine every morning' (Samuel Pepys' diary, 1665). Carrying a rabbit's or hare's foot about was generally considered to be lucky. Wearing rabbit-skin socks inside shoes was thought specifically to prevent chest troubles.

Speed

Unlike the hare, which clocks up to 80 kph/50 mph, the rabbit is not a very fast runner. Although, over the first few metres it is faster than the hare, it quickly tires and loses to the hare, which has far more stamina, over long distances.

The rabbit dashes and scampers and seeks the safety of a burrow rather than trying to outrun a pursuer; nevertheless, over short distances on open ground, it can touch 38 kph/24 mph.

It is, however, quite a neat swimmer. The marsh and swamp rabbits of the Americas and the West Indies take to the water with gay abandon. Surprisingly, rabbits can also climb quite well and they are found living in the thatched roofs of Hebridean cottages. They get a grip on account of the hair on the undersurface of their feet.

Biology

The digestive system

The digestive system of the rabbit is specially adapted to the processing of large quantities of vegetable matter (a 2-kg/4-lb rabbit can easily eat over 0.5 kg/1 lb food each day). Rabbits possess chisel-shaped front teeth (incisors) for gnawing their food. Behind the long, constantly growing front incisors there is another pair of short peg-like incisors which provide a 'bite' for the lower incisors. The cheek teeth or molars have sharply ridged surfaces. The ridges of the upper molars fit perfectly into those of the lower ones, providing an excellent grinding mechanism for finely chopping plant food.

To aid digestion, rabbits have a large cul-de-sac, called a caecum, situated in their bowels. It lies between the small and large intestines and ends in a prominent appendix, resembling that of a human being although rabbits seldom suffer from appendicitis! Some other mammals also possess appendices, but they are usually very small and non-functional. Rabbit appendices, however, do seem to be important organs, perhaps involved in digestion and certainly helping, by means of their abundant lymphatic tissue, to fight off bowel infections.

Did you know?

All over Britain there exists the luck-bringing custom of saying 'rabbits' or 'white rabbits' once or three times on the first day of the month.

The caecum itself teems with 'good' bacteria which act as microscopic workers dissolving the outer cellulose and making the nutriments within plant tissue available to the rabbit. These nutriments are partly

Refection

One might assume that the products of digestion would be lost by the rabbit and merely lie on the ground, wasted. Not so, however. The rabbit has a trick up his sleeve! Rabbits exhibit a phenomenon known as refection. They eat some of their droppings, not the usual blackish hard pellets, but the lighter-coloured soft ones which are passed during the day in nocturnal species and during the night in those active by day, such as domesticated rabbits. So their digestive systems have a second chance to work on and absorb goodies from their food.

Because it happens usually at night, you may seldom see your pet rabbit eating his special droppings. Some rabbits are very quick at doing it and will even gobble down the pellets just as they emerge from the anus. Remember that a rabbit refecting in this way is acting perfectly normally. It is not 'being dirty', and hasn't 'got worms'!

Refection and the part played by bacteria in digesting the rabbit's food are the equivalent of rumination (cud-chewing) in animals such as cows and sheep, which also rely on resident populations of microbes in their innards to aid digestion.

absorbed through the intestine wall and enter the blood stream, but some pass out with the droppings. They include important quantities of the essential vitamin B12 which is synthesized in the bowels.

Internal organs

Apart from the design of the gastro-intestinal system the rabbit's innards are much like those of other mammals. Like us, it has a heart, lungs, liver, kidneys, bladder and so forth — indeed, it is just as intricately and amazingly constructed as you or me.

Fur

The glory of the rabbit is, of course, its fur coat. This is composed of two types of hair in most breeds: long, strong guard hairs and an undercoat. Guard hairs are shorter than the undercoat hairs in Rex rabbits, but both types are luxuriously long in Angoras.

Some domestic rabbits produce different coat colours depending upon their environmental temperature. Himalayans, for example, do not develop their black markings if kept at temperatures above 28°C/84°F.

In newborn rabbits, the first hairs to grow are guard hairs but, within days, the undercoat hairs appear and a delightfully soft 'baby coat' is then in place. It lasts for four to six weeks and is then gradually replaced by the intermediate coat, a process that is completed by five to six months of age. The formation of the third coat occurs in adult rabbits, usually twice a year, but there are exceptions. The time of moulting depends on a variety of factors, including age, sexual activity, other hormonal influences, and especially the season of the year.

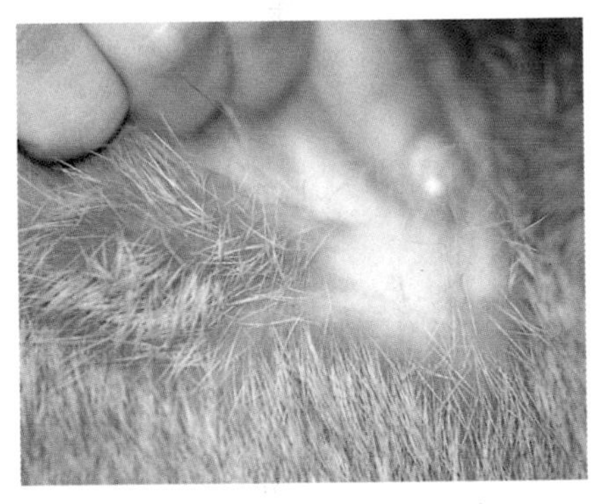

Above: *Below the rabbit's long guard hairs is a dense undercoat.*

Moulting begins normally at the front of the body, with the head, and proceeds backwards and downwards. In most cases the first, somewhat heavier, moult is in March or April (in the northern hemisphere) with the more substantial winter coat being lost. The lighter summer coat is shed in autumn.

So-called 'extra' moults may occur as when a pregnant doe lines her nest with fur plucked from her underparts or when stimulated by hormones if she goes into false or pseudo-pregnancy.

CHAPTER FOUR

Acquiring a rabbit

Finding the right rabbit for you. A difficult choice? Certainly, there are so many breeds and varieties, all of which are admirable, but how do you make up your mind which one to choose?

Although your decision will be partly subjective, from the heart, when you just 'click' with a particular bright-eyed, nose-a-twitch bundle of fur, there are a number of criteria that you must decide upon when selecting a rabbit. Some criteria apply to the rabbit while others relate to you, your family, your house and your circumstances.

Housing your rabbit

Firstly, do you want a pet rabbit kept in the time-honoured way in a hutch in the garden or in the house, rather like a dog or cat? There is much more about the house rabbit later (see page 74). Particularly in the case of house rabbits, do you have young children and/or other pets?

Children and pets

Children of pre-school age are best advised to wait until they are older before being given rabbits. Young children can upset and exhaust rabbits by bad or persistent handling of them. Even older

children should not be put in charge of caring for rabbits unless they fully understand the animals' daily needs and you are sure that they will not soon tire of their pets. It takes a lot of time and patience to ensure that cats, dogs and rabbits get on peaceably together; it is more difficult when a rabbit is brought into the already established territory of a cat or dog. Jealousy will out! However, peaceful coexistence can be achieved.

Usually rabbits and guinea-pigs can be kept together — if their quarters are sufficiently spacious. Where they are kept in relatively cramped conditions, or if a rabbit, particularly a buck, is a stroppy, jealous character, the guinea-pig can get literally squashed or stamped to death.

Did you know?

Matthew Hopkins, the Witch Finder General of early seventeenth-century England, swore on oath that he had personally seen two witches' 'familiars' in the form of black rabbits named Sack and Sugar while interrogating and keeping awake for four nights a suspected witch, Elizabeth Clark. She was subsequently convicted and hanged.

How many rabbits and what sex?

Do you want one or two rabbits? It is not cruel to keep one rabbit alone. They are normally completely happy provided that they get regular human attention. However, as with other species, I think it is best if you can keep a pair. If you decide on such a duo, try to obtain litter mates or, at least, animals of the same age. If the

Below: *This cuddly threesome obviously get on well together.*

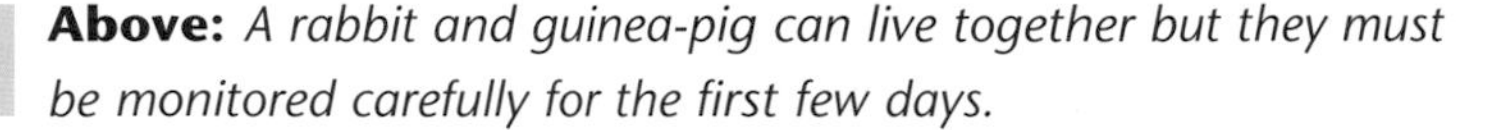

Above: *A rabbit and guinea-pig can live together but they must be monitored carefully for the first few days.*

pair consists of a male and a female and you are not prepared to cope correctly, and repeatedly, with the patter of tiny rabbit feet, then it is best to have the buck castrated. Such non-reproductive pairs are, in my view, ideal for most pet owners.

Two buck rabbits will fight after they attain sexual maturity at about four months of age; these scraps can end in serious wounding. Two does, particularly if they come from the same litter, will live harmoniously together all their lives.

If you want a house rabbit, a doe is best; males begin spraying urine, rather like tom cats, after sexual maturity unless castrated.

Other considerations

Have you got the right place, housing and equipment ready for your pet? Are there any regulations in your home town restricting or even banning the keeping of rabbits, as sometimes happens in the United States? Have you time to tend your rabbit daily? Who will look after the rabbit when you go on holiday?

CHAPTER
FOUR

Most important of all among the human criteria for rabbit-keeping, do you know anything about or have you had previous experience of owning such creatures? If not, read this book and talk to a rabbit breeder, a member of a local rabbit club, or your veterinary surgeon first.

Did you know?

There are still many superstitions concerning rabbits. Fishermen going to their boats or miners on their way to the pit traditionally consider that seeing a rabbit is a bad omen.

Choosing a rabbit

Now we must consider the factors governing your choice that involve the rabbit itself.

1 Where from?

It is best to buy a rabbit from a reputable pet shop or a breeder whose premises and stock look clean and in good condition. Pet shop rabbits will normally be cross-bred 'mongrels' but are none the worse pets for that. They make just as good friends as pedigree stock and are, perhaps, best for beginners.

2 How old?

It is best to obtain young rabbits but *not* ones that are too young and have been taken away from their mothers prematurely, and cruelly, at four to five weeks of age. The youngster should be at least eight weeks old and should be fully weaned on to solid food.

3 If a pedigree, what breed?

All rabbits, all breeds, any type of 'mongrel' are suitable as pets and can, with good handling, give years of friendship, pleasure, interest and fascination. In the end, you pay your money and you make your choice! But note the following:

- Dwarf rabbits — these are much loved by children. They are cute little animals weighing up to 1.5 kg/3 lb. Some, however, are difficult to housetrain.

■ Angoras — they need shearing every three months and demand daily grooming.

■ French Lops — they can be grumpy, bad tempered and untidy in their hutches.

■ Van Beverens — these rabbits can be peevish and are best not for children.

■ Dutch and English — these are two examples of hardy breeds; both are easy to keep.

■ Lilac, Dutch, English, New Zealand White and Himalayan — these are five examples of very docile breeds.

Basically, pet rabbits are what you make them, no matter the breed. Good, regular handling and proper care will guarantee an excellent, amiable and attentive pet.

Below: *Rabbits can be a great source of interest and can give you and your family many years of pleasure.*

CHAPTER
FOUR

Selecting your pet

Before handling a prospective new pet, watch it carefully for a while. Is it alert and bright-eyed? It may be rather shy and retreat into a corner or it may inspect you with nose-twitching, prick-eared curiosity — either form of behaviour is normal, but the animal should not be dull and apathetic. You should handle the animal and check the following points.

- Examine the ears which should be ever mobile — is there any dark discharge or flaky, 'cheesy' material within them?

- Are the eyes and ears free of discharge. Is there any white or coloured 'matter'? Any signs of reddening that could be inflammation? Any overflowing tears?

- Does it cough or sneeze?

- Inspect each foot — are the toes, the skin between them, and the nails clean and dry with no evidence of weeping ulcers or inflamed areas?

- Is the rabbit's fur coat smooth and with an overall gentle shine?

Don't be misled!

The rabbit must be absolutely normal in all the above aspects. Ignore any excuses or explanations given by the seller — 'She always sneezes after I put new hay in' or 'Don't worry about the bald patches — it's just finished moulting.' If you have any doubts at all, don't accept the rabbit or, at least, get a vet's opinion before you buy it.

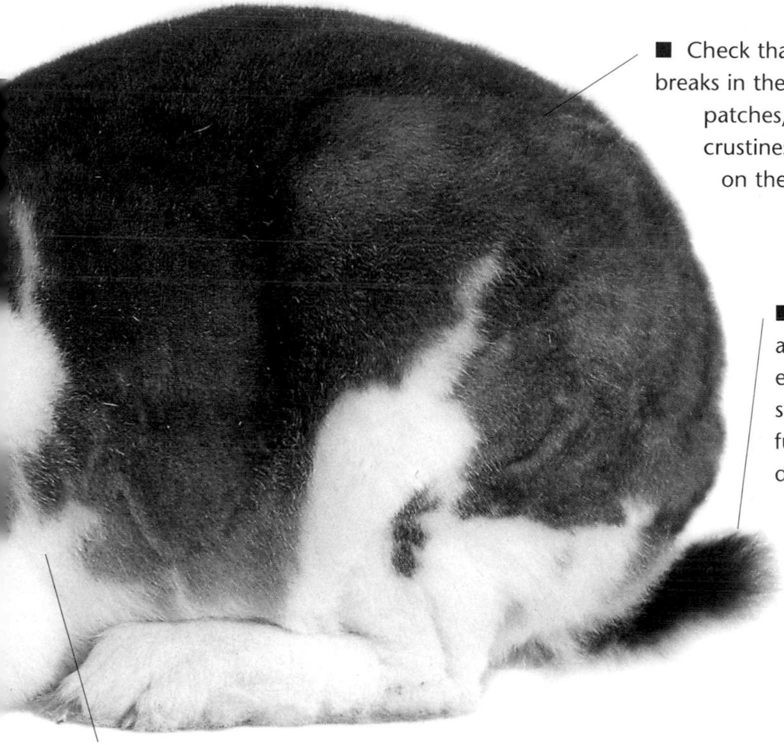

■ Check that there are no breaks in the fur, no bare patches, no feelings of crustiness, lumps or spots on the skin.

■ Look under the tail at the fur of the back end. Are there any signs of soiling of the fur that might indicate diarrhoea?

❖ *Dalmation Rex*

■ Put the palm of your hand under the rabbit's belly and squeeze very, very gently. The abdomen should be relaxed, soft and in proportion to the rabbit's size, not swollen, tense, or hard. **Note:** Never squeeze the belly of a heavily pregnant doe!

CHAPTER FIVE

Housing your rabbit

Good housing, together with a correct diet, is the key to a long life and happiness for the pet rabbit. As with the acquisition of human dwellings, rabbit accommodation needs to be carefully worked out in advance.

The criteria to be considered in providing your bunny or bunnies with a home are freedom from damp and draughts, and space together with snugness, sanitation and security.

Outdoors

Outdoors premises for your rabbit, or rabbits, will comprise a properly constructed hutch of adequate size together with an exercise run. This is important as hutch life alone without the opportunity to exercise is no life for your pet. Would you like to live all your life in just two rooms of your house?

Hutch designs

The rabbit's hutch should be well made of strong timber at least 1 cm/½ in thick, and have two compartments: the living room and the bedroom, or nesting box. Both compartments should permit the rabbit to lie down fully stretched in any direction and

Above: *This rabbit hutch is large enough for two rabbits to live comfortably together.*

to stand on its hind legs without touching the ceiling.

- There should be a pitched roof sloping backwards with an overhang at the front, covered with a tough waterproof material.
- There should be a strong wire mesh front to one side of the living room, about 80 cm/2 ft 8 in high.
- The hutch should have legs to raise it off the ground.

Minimum hutch sizes – outdoors

The minimum dimensions are as follows:

Small rabbit	(e.g. Netherlands Dwarf) 90 x 60 x 45 cm/3 x 2 x 1½ ft high
Medium rabbit	(e.g. Dutch) 120 x 60 x 60 cm/4 x 2 x 2 ft high
Large rabbit	(e.g. Californian, Vienna Blue) 150 x 60 x 60 cm/5 x 2 x 2 ft high
Giant rabbit	(e.g. Flemish Giant) 180 x 75 x 75 cm/6 x 2½ x 2½ ft high

More than one rabbit: add 30 cm/1 ft in width per rabbit

Above: *A rabbit must have a partitioned hutch with room to stretch out flat in both the living room and bedroom.*

- Always allow enough room for the animal(s) to grow.
- The interior should be given a smooth finish — I prefer Formica.
- The nesting box must be big enough to allow the rabbit(s) to stretch out on its (their) sides.
- The solid floor should be protected by coating with polyurethane to make it watertight, and provided with a shallow galvanized tray containing a 5-cm/2-in deep layer of litter, or the floor can be covered by a suitable litter (see page 71).
- Wire mesh floors are undesirable; they

Right: *A hutch must be raised off the ground to prevent damp getting in.*

reduce cleaning, of course, but are very hard on the rabbit's feet.

- Any wood preservatives used must be nontoxic.
- Hay or straw should be provided in the rabbit's sleeping compartment, which is fitted with a draft-proof solid door. Side doors are far better than hatches in the roof or removable roofs. In the wild, predators tend to seize rabbits from above and, instinctively, domestic rabbits can be alarmed by hands approaching suddenly from on high.
- A wooden panel with ventilation holes or a curtain of thick sacking should be attachable in front of the living room mesh for use in adverse weather conditions such as driving rain and excessive cold.

Did you know?

A rabbit warren can have between one and 150 entrances.

Temperature range

Rabbits prefer a temperature range of 10–18°C/47–64°F, but are somewhat hardy outside these limits. However, you should beware of temperatures above 28°C/84°F; when it becomes this hot there is a strong risk of heat exhaustion with possibly fatal results. Should the temperature exceed 28°C/84°F, your rabbit should be moved to a cooler location or brought indoors if you have air conditioning or a cool garage or basement.

The ideal hutch location

The best direction for positioning the rabbit's hutch is towards the south-east, not facing directly into the wind or sun. Placing the hutch in the shade and against a protective wall or fence is always a wise measure.

Be aware that wild and domestic animals may attempt to access your garden and attack your pet. Therefore, make sure that the hutch is secure and protected from predators.

Transporting a rabbit

Whenever you transport a rabbit, use a proper carrier. Small dog or cat boxes, available at the pet shop, are ideal. Do not carry a rabbit in a wire cage; if the animal jumps around it may cut its feet. The British Rabbit Council and the American Rabbit Breeders Association produce lists of correct sizes for carriers for each rabbit breed. If transporting a rabbit by car in warm weather, beware of hyperthermia caused by poor ventilation or solar radiation through the windows. Make your journey time as short as possible and always keep the vehicle interior cool, particularly when the car is stationary.

Litter

For the floor of the hutch or litter box there are a number of suitable types of litter. Some rabbits will prefer one to another, and rabbits with a tendency to sore hocks (heels) should be provided with the softer kinds. Cages and hutches must be cleaned out twice or three times weekly as

Right: *Protect the floor of the hutch with sheets of polyurethane and newspaper, a layer of wood flakes and then the hay. This prevents the hay becoming damp and mouldy.*

rabbits urinate abundantly. It's a good idea to put a layer of newspaper under the litter. This makes for easier cleaning out.

Furnishing the hutch

You will need to install the following in the hutch:

1 A wire or wooden hayrack.

2 A glazed earthenware or stainless steel food bowl (not a plastic one which can be knocked over easily and is chewable).

3 A water bottle with a ball valve which is hung on the wire mesh (not a water bowl which can be contaminated easily). Exercise runs must also be provided at all times with water bottles.

4 A gnawing block. Sometimes rabbits may chew at their hutch woodwork in order to wear down their teeth. You can avoid this by providing a bark-covered log for use as a gnawing block.

Did you know?

Working in suitable soil, a wild rabbit can excavate two metres of burrow in one night. Yes, you've guessed it — who does most of the digging? The female, of course!

Scrubbing the hutch

As well as cleaning out and tidying the hutch at least two or three times weekly, it should be scrubbed out thoroughly once a week. Remove

Above: *Types of commonly available rabbit litter:* ***1*** *Hay;* ***2*** *Dust-extracted shredded barley straw;* ***3*** *Shredded newspaper;* ***4*** *Straw;* ***5*** *Wood flakes.*

Suitable litter for rabbits

Litter type	Advantages	Disadvantages.
Hay and straw	Dust-extracted hay and straw are best (less risk of mites and moulds). It is acceptable, even desirable, if a rabbit eats this litter.	Both can be messy. Barley straw has spiky seed husks that can prick and injure rabbits' paws and is best avoided.
Dried grass	Good and edible.	Can be expensive.
Peat	Good and absorbent.	Does look rather 'dirty'.
Hemp plant litter	Clean and absorbent, resistant to mites, and biodegradable. Made from the core of the hemp plant.	Best not eaten by the animal.
Corncob litter	Excellent, clean and absorbent.	Fairly expensive. Change frequently to avoid mould.
Shredded newspaper	This is OK.	Don't use it if the rabbit tends to eat it.
Wood pulp, citrus peel, rice hull and aspen shavings, proprietary litters	All of these are excellent, clean, absorbent and biodegradable.	None.
Clay, clumping-type cat litter	Do *not* use this for rabbits. It tends to be ingested when the rabbit grooms itself and can lead to intestinal obstruction or other serious conditions.	
Non-clumping cat litters	Suitable for rabbits.	None.
Softwood beddings (pine shavings, sawdust, chips)	Best to avoid these products because of their variable content of phenolic chemicals. They can cause anything from eye and nose irritation to respiratory disease, immuno-deficiency or liver damage.	

the rabbit before scrubbing and then use a brush and a weak solution of household bleach in water, an organic iodine disinfectant appropriately diluted, or the type of disinfectant used for glassware and kitchen equipment but not the phenolic type which is usually black and goes white when mixed with water. The hutch must be completely dry before reintroducing its occupant.

Exercise runs

Daily exercise, either indoors or outdoors, is essential in keeping a rabbit fit, healthy and happy. For outside use, your rabbit will require a portable exercise pen, with minimum dimensions of 120 x 240 cm/4 x 8 ft. Tent-shaped or rectangular with a flat roof, the pen should be constructed of well galvanized 40-mm mesh wire. The wire must never be thinner than 1.5 mm. There should be a rigid wooden 'skirting board' and a wire mesh floor. Cover one end to afford the rabbit some shelter from the sun. Moving the pen around frequently prevents the ground within the run becoming 'sick' (overloaded with parasites or bacteria).

Burrowing outside is seldom any problem, but be aware that ingesting too much grass, particularly in the spring, can lead to digestive upsets in a rabbit. Never leave your pet unattended in its run as predators or vermin may try to attack.

Left: *If your garden isn't 'rabbit friendly' you can train most rabbits to use a special rabbit lead.*

'Happy families'

In the streets of early Victorian London, some folk scratched a living by exhibiting so-called 'Happy Families' where animals of a variety of species were kept together, ostensibly amicably, in one cage. Rabbits would be displayed cheek by jowl with cats, dogs, monkeys, magpies, hawks, owls and sewer rats. One fellow boasted to the social investigator Mayhew that such a motley collection 'has once gone thirty-six hours, as a trial, without food — that was in Cambridge and no creature was injured; but they were very peckish, especially the birds of prey.' He claimed that 'hundreds have tried their hands at "Happy Families", and have failed .... It's principally done, however, I may tell you, by continued kindness, and petting and studying the nature of the creatures.' We certainly hope so!

Below: *Portable runs come in a variety of shapes and sizes. Make sure they are completely enclosed with wire mesh to prevent predators getting in. A covered area or cardboard box in the run offers a nervous rabbit a protective 'bolt hole' in which to retreat.*

CHAPTER
FIVE

Indoors: the house rabbit

A rapidly increasing number of rabbit lovers are keeping their pets indoors, in some ways just like domestic dogs or cats. To do this you will need an indoor cage which will constitute bunny's 'home within the home' — its headquarters and bedroom. Suitable metal cages can be bought at a pet shop. The cage should have a removable top and a wide door and can be fitted either with an underfloor tray or equipped with a litter box. Even if you are buying a baby rabbit, you should plan out its accommodation according to its potential adult size. Later, with experience, it may be that you will wish to alter, extend and perhaps glamorize your pet's quarters with a bespoke construction of some kind.

Minimum cage sizes – indoors

The size of the cage is important and I recommend the following minimum floor space area for various sizes of animal:

Up to 1.8 kg/4 lb	(e.g. Dwarf rabbits) 45 cm^2/ 1½ sq ft
1.8–3.6 kg/4–8 lb	(e.g. Dutch, Havana, Rex) 92 cm^2/3 sq ft
3.6–5.4 kg/8–12 lb	(e.g. Flemish Giant) 153 cm^2/5 sq ft
Over 5.4 kg/12 lb	(e.g. Giant Papillon, Blanc de Bouscat) 153 cm^2/5 sq ft
Height of cage:	Minimum height for all sizes of rabbit is 38 cm/15 in

Note: In the United States, the Federal Animal Welfare Act demands that a large adult rabbit must be provided with at least 114 cm^2/4 square feet of cage floor space and a cage height of at least 35.5 cm/14 in.

Cage furniture

Furniture for the rabbit's cage should include the following items:

- A hanging automatic valve water bottle.
- A solid (glazed earthenware or stainless steel) feeding bowl (a hanging one will save space).
- A suitable litter box, about 25 x 30 cm/10 x 12 in for one rabbit, or 37.5 x 50 cm/15 x 20 in for two rabbits.
- Litter, as described for the outdoor rabbit (see page 71).
- A rug, e.g. synthetic fur, sheepskin, etc., to lie on.
- Rabbit toys, e.g. hard plastic balls, toilet paper spools and cardboard boxes.
- A second litter box, 37.5 x 50 cm/15 x 20 in, will be required for the floor of the cage when the rabbit is let out to run free.

Above: *Rabbits, like most pets, need stimulation. This can be provided with 'toys' such as cardboard boxes and toilet paper spools. Food can be hidden in them to encourage your rabbit to use its well-developed senses.*

Location and cleaning

Indoor rabbit cages should be positioned away from all draughts, fireplaces or other sources of heat, dark corners and machinery, such as washing machines, dishwashers, television sets and radios. Rabbits are extremely sensitive to draughts and also to certain irritating mechanical or electronic noises, some of which their ears pick up while ours cannot. An ideal spot for the cage would be one that is off of the main thoroughfare used by the human inhabitants of the house, which is peaceful but not totally isolated from all activity, is well-lit but not in direct sunlight, and which has a steady environmental temperature in the range of 12–22°C/55–75°F.

Rabbits can withstand colder temperatures better than hotter ones. Remember always that if you have small children, that the rabbit's cage is its private quarters. It should be able to relax and rest there when it chooses. Discourage toddlers from wanting to pick up and extract the rabbit from its domain whenever they feel the urge. Rabbits, particularly the winsome Dwarves, are not toys.

As with outdoor hutches, the rabbit's indoor cage must be cleaned regularly, the exact frequency depending on how much time the animal spends at large in the house. Usually once or twice a week is enough and all that is required is dusting, vacuuming and sponging with a weak solution of a non-phenolic disinfectant (the kind used around the kitchen) in water. Soiled litter should be replaced every two days or so.

Left: *If you house your rabbit indoors in a wooden hutch, make sure the wooden floor is protected by sheets of polyurethane and newspaper with hay on top.*

Introducing a rabbit into its new home

Firstly, before bringing your new pet home, you should make sure that its accommodation is fully prepared — a comfortable, snug bed, litter in place, water bottle and hay rack filled, and a tempting mixture of grains, apple, broccoli (calabrese), parsley and dandelion leaves in the food dish.

When it arrives, put the rabbit into its hutch or cage and leave it alone for a couple of hours, keeping excited children and dumbfounded dogs and cats well away from it while it settles in to its new home.

With house rabbits it is best to keep them in their cage, except when brought out for some daily handling and petting, for two or three weeks. Then they can be allowed out, not at first with the freedom to roam around the entire house but into what can be called a 'beginner's space'. This is a small area of a room, porch or hallway that is enclosed by means of wooden, plastic or wire mesh barriers. A baby pen is ideal or perhaps you can block

Safety in the home

Before giving bunny the keys to your house, check for dangers.

1 If the rabbit has access to terraces or balconies it may fall to its death or be targeted by marauding cats. Put wire mesh to a height of at least 90 cm/3 ft along balustrades or railings to prevent falls. As for cats, don't let your rabbit enter vulnerable areas without constant supervision.

2 Check that electrical wires, telephone cords, house plants and delicate Meissen porcelain, etc. are out of nudge-and-nibble reach by inquisitive rabbits. Cover things, rearrange furniture to prevent access and try repeated light applications of the pet repellent sprays used for dogs and cats.

off a suitable corner with plastic baby gates. Some pet stores stock purpose-built, collapsible rabbit play pens.

Cover the floor of the 'beginner's space' with matting (seagrass is excellent) and put in stable, non-chewable water and food receptacles, a litter box and a selection of rabbit toys and chews. Some rabbits are fussy about using their litter box; you may have to move its position within the space or even add a second litter box.

During the first few weeks confined to its cage or hutch, the rabbit will begin to train itself to use its litter box. If it starts by sleeping on its litter box, add more luxury to the floor of the cage or hutch bedroom, providing a patch of sheepskin. Most rabbits prefer ultra-comfortable beds!

The rabbit will mark its new territory in the time-honoured manner with samples of droppings and urine. Hopefully this will be done in its litterbox. To begin with, you can teach your rabbit to do this as soon as you release it from its cage by

Tips on housetraining

■ Before you first let a rabbit out of its cage, put some of its own droppings into the litter box in the 'beginner's space'.

■ Place the litter box in one of the rabbit's favourite places in the room.

■ Let the animal out of its cage several times a day (say, for fifteen to twenty minutes per time).

■ If possible, let it out before feeding. Feeding stimulates a defaecation reflex.

■ If the rabbit passes droppings on the floor, pick them up at once and place them in the litter box. It will get the idea eventually!

■ Swab the floor where droppings or urine have been passed with white vinegar. Rabbits hate the smell, and the vinegar also acts as a mild disinfectant and neutralizer of the very alkaline rabbit urine.

Right: *Older children find that house rabbits make wonderful pets.*

popping it immediately on to the 'beginner's space' litter box. If you then fill a large plastic container with hay, it can serve as both litter box and 'chew'. The rabbit will use one side as a toilet and chomp hay happily on the other — rabbits are very clean people!

After a few weeks, although older rabbits may take longer, and once the rabbit has become fond of using its litter box, you can allow it to explore further into the home. The litter box (or boxes) remain in the place or places that the animal has become accustomed to finding them. Spayed and neutered rabbits housetrain more rapidly than 'un-doctored' ones.

Meeting dogs and cats

It can be tricky introducing a new puppy or kitten into a household where there are already one or more dogs or cats in residence. Territory, pride, jealousy, incompatability all come into play in the short term. A new rabbit, especially one allowed to roam freely, creates the extra dimension of potential trouble in its role as a prey animal expected to mix amicably with carnivorous predators. So how do you do it?

CHAPTER
FIVE

Holiday time

It is most important to plan for the care and maintenance of your rabbit when you go on holiday. Arrange if possible for someone, say a member of your local rabbit club or another rabbit owner, to come in on a daily basis to attend to your pet. If you ask a neighbour who has little or no experience of these animals, leave detailed, preferably written, instructions on cleaning, feeding, watering, etc., together with the telephone numbers of your vet and your holiday destination.

With cats

1 Keep the rabbit in its cage and allow the cat into the room. Stroke the cat and make a fuss of it, praising it, as it inspects the newcomer. If it tries to claw at the rabbit, scold it firmly. If it persists, spray it with short bursts from a water pistol. Repeat this process frequently.

2 Sit with both pets on your lap. Let them sniff one another. Repeat the process frequently.

3 Finally, let the rabbit hop about in or out of doors with the cat on a lead. When the cat gets bored with this hopping novelty and no longer pulls to pursue it, you've won. Repeat the process frequently until the desired result occurs.

With dogs

1 Keep the rabbit in its cage and bring the dog into the room. Praise the dog and pet it as it inspects the newcomer. Scold it if it barks. Repeat this process frequently.

2 Place the rabbit on your lap and sit in such a way that the dog and rabbit are at eye level. Allow the dog to sniff and lick the rabbit. Scold and pull on the dog's collar if it tries to misbehave. Pet and praise both animals continually and equally. Repeat the process frequently.

3 Let the rabbit run free and hold the dog on a lead. Praise and pet the dog and only release it if it shows no urge to chase the rabbit. Repeat the process as necessary.

With another rabbit in your home

1 Keep each rabbit in its cage. Place the cages next to one another. Repeat a few times.
2 Keep the new rabbit in its cage and let the other one out. It may circle round the newcomer's cage leaving scent marks — don't worry, that's OK.
3 Hold both rabbits on your lap, petting both equally. Let them sniff one another. Keep a firm grasp on the dominant individual to prevent biting.
4 Let both rabbits run free with lots of space. Supervise them carefully and separate them if biting progresses beyond gentle nipping.

Did you know?

Some ostrich farms in Europe are using rabbits as companions to keep young ostriches happy and content. Dwarf varieties of rabbit make the best 'nannies' for the youngest birds, but as the ostriches grow bigger and stroppier, heftier types, such as the Flemish Giant, are more able to deal with their charges.

Above: *Dogs and rabbits can learn to get on well. This pair seem a little doubtful, the dog more so than the rabbit.*

CHAPTER SIX

Looking after your rabbit

Rabbits are easily frightened and must always be handled with care. They must never be shouted at, smacked or physically chastised in any way. If badly handled, rabbits can struggle violently and may thereby injure their spinal cords, perhaps seriously. Severe fear and stress can even induce a fatal heart attack in any small pet.

Did you know?

Angora wool is the lightest and softest of all animal fibres. One thousand metres of yarn can be spun from a mere seven grammes of good Angora wool. Almost three times the weight of fine grade sheep's wool would be needed to provide the same length of yarn.

Handling your rabbit

Forget the magician's old stunt of plucking a rabbit out of his top hat by its ears. It's no way to handle the animal. Never, ever pick a rabbit up by its ears. If it is nervous or fractious, you should grasp the scruff with one hand and support the rabbit's rump with the palm of your other hand.

Tamer pet rabbits may not like the indignity of being 'scruffed'. With such an individual, put one hand under the chest, holding each foreleg separately between the thumb and two fingers, and, as above, take the weight with your other hand under the rump. When carrying a rabbit thus held, keep it close

CHAPTER
SIX

to your chest. The animal is then best placed on a solid nonslip surface, such as a table, but still restrained by your hands.

Grooming your rabbit

Rabbits are smart in more ways than one. They keep their furry coat in perfect condition by fastidiously grooming themselves. There is only one exception — the Angora.

All other rabbit breeds need little in the way of hairdressing. Regular brushing (twice a week) with a medium stiff brush is recommended, especially during the moulting season. As well as removing dead hair it stimulates blood circulation in the skin and is pleasurable to the rabbit. The grooming sessions also give you the opportunity to check for any fur and skin abnormalities. Any

Right: *The Angora's fur grows so long that it needs regular stripping.*
Below: *It is essential to brush an Angora rabbit's coat every day.*

Right: *For docile pet rabbits, it is always preferable to pick them up without scruffing them.*

soiled areas of the coat, perhaps around the anus or genital opening, can be cleaned gently with a soft cloth dipped in some warm water or a little olive oil or by means of talcum powder or a piece of white bread.

Angora rabbits have a unique soft coat that can grow to be over 12.5 cm/5 in long. They must be brushed thoroughly every day, beginning when they are about five weeks of age, never earlier. Friendly and cooperative, Angoras are happy to be groomed regularly. It isn't essential, but if you are interested in collecting the fabulous Angora wool, they should be sheared or plucked by an expert once every three months.

Teeth and nails

Each week check your rabbit's teeth to see if they are growing too long and do the same with its toe nails. Overgrown teeth should be dealt with by the veterinary surgeon (see page 108). If a rabbit's claws become overgrown, the excess nails can be trimmed off. This is best done by your vet, especially in

Left: *Claws as long as these need trimming to prevent damage to the rabbit and its owner.*

dark-coloured rabbits with dark nails. If you feel competent to trim a pale-coloured rabbit's overgrown claws, use 'guillotine-type' animal nail clippers, which are obtainable from pet stores — they are much better than the human-type clippers.

You should be able to see the pink core, or 'quick', of the claw through the translucent shell. This is where the blood vessels and nerves run. Cut at least 1 cm/½ in in front of the tip of the quick.

Feeding your rabbit

Rabbits certainly eat! Their rapid spread across Australia, New Zealand and Chile resulted in the devastation of pastures, the ruin of sheep farmers and the erosion of land. In Britain, too, particularly in the nineteenth century, rabbits have done serious damage to crops, woodland and grassland. In 1937, a select committee of the House of Lords stated that 'the rabbit has seldom been killed which, on sale, did not owe somebody several shillings as a result of its depredations'.

Wild rabbits will eat almost anything. They munch the poisonous foxglove and deadly nightshade (dangerous for pet rabbits) without any ill effects, but tend to leave the less poisonous

Feeding tips

- It is important to establish a routine feeding schedule: do not vary the times of feedings and do not make sudden changes in the quantity or types of foods fed.
- Never feed your rabbit any of the dangerous and poisonous plants that are listed on page 94.
- Make sure that the food is at room temperature; never give food directly from the refrigerator.

ragwort alone. They don't like azalea, rhododendron, honeysuckle, hawthorn, dogwood, sorrel, comfrey (enjoyed by many a pet rabbit), burdock, cowslip or primrose and will usually eat nettles only when food is scarce.

Did you know?

Curiously, rabbits seem to detest the cuckoo pint or arum, and yet this plant is also called *pain de lievre*, or hare's bread, supposedly a staple ingredient of the hare's diet.

Pet rabbit food

Like other mammals and human beings, rabbits need a diet containing proteins for growth, carbohydrates and fats for energy, vitamins and minerals for a host of chemical processes within the body, fibre for healthy functioning of the digestive tract, and water without which few living organisms can survive for long. They prefer high-protein, high-carbohydrate, low-fibre potions of plants when given a choice, and are fastidious, even fussy, eaters to whom, like human gourmets, the smell, form and texture of food is extremely important.

There are several ways of feeding a pet rabbit for maximum

Below: *Rabbits can easily suffer from malnutrition through incorrect feeding.*

health and condition but the best, in my opinion, is to use a basic core of balanced, nutritionally complete rabbit pellets with good timothy hay supplemented by judicious quantities of fresh vegetables (especially green ones), concentrates such as cereals, and an unlimited, constant supply of fresh drinking water. Variety is the spice of life for rabbits and they thrive best on a varied, interesting diet, but the owner has to monitor the situation at all times — overfeeding of some foods can lead to unwelcome obesity, and food intake is, as with you and me, also related to the amount of exercise taken by the rabbit. The most common

Above: *Commonly available foods and supplements for rabbits:* ***1*** *Fresh vegetables;* ***2*** *Vegetable sticks with seeds, enriched with vitamins and minerals;* ***3*** *Mineral stone;* ***4*** *Vegetable drops enriched with vitamins and minerals;* ***5*** *Dry rabbit pellets;* ***6*** *Vegetable supplements to dry food;* ***7*** *Complete rabbit mix.*

feeding regime for pet rabbits is to use a 'complete' specially compounded rabbit food which is available commercially, and usually in the form of pellets. Although the average medium-sized rabbit will eat about 170 g/6 oz of pellets daily, it has been found that feeding less pellets, e.g. 60–90 g/2–3 oz, and feeding timothy hay free-choice (as much as the rabbit wants), is often better in preventing common rabbit health problems, such as obesity, digestive upsets and hair chewing. If using this regime, it is important to feed timothy hay, not alfalfa hay, as alfalfa hay is too high in calcium to be fed in large quantities to rabbits and might promote problems with crystal formation in the urinary tract.

Fresh greens

Rabbits have a very sensitive digestive tract microflora (bacterial population) which is easily upset by sudden indiscriminate feeding, such as offering oats, cookies, rabbit treat mixes, or too many fresh greens, Although fresh greens can and should be fed, they should only be offered in the morning in small quantities of no more than 10–20 g/less than an ounce a day so that the rabbit can digest them properly.

Dry foods

Cereals, grains, seeds and stale (but not mouldy) bread are sometimes called concentrated or dry foods. These items are full of carbohydrate and, in some cases, fat

Fresh greens

Good choices of fresh greens for rabbits include the following:

- Beet greens
- Brussels sprouts
- Broccoli
- Cabbage
- Carrots and carrot tops
- Celery
- Chicory
- Kale
- Parsley
- Parsnips
- Snow peas
- Spinach

Note: Feed kale and spinach very sparingly and avoid beans, potato sprouts, maize and rhubarb.

- Lettuce is not a very valuable food for rabbits and it might, under certain circumstances, dope them! Curiously the authoress, Beatrix Potter in her 'Tale of the Flopsy Bunnies', published in 1909, wrote of the soporific effect of lettuce on young rabbits.

CHAPTER SIX

Recommended daily dry food

I suggest the following amounts of dry food as maxima per day.

Large breeds	40 g/1½ oz
Medium breeds	25 g/1 oz
Small breeds	15 g/½ oz

You can feed these plus the hay and green food but as an alternative to the complete food pellets. I like to feed the complete pellets on some days and the dry food on others.

energy (e.g. sunflower seeds) can easily be overfed. Obesity can lead to disease, infertility and death. However, these foods can be used to advantage when, say, a doe is lactating and needs extra calories; and linseed and sunflower seeds, fed sparingly, bring a fine sheen to the rabbit's coat.

Water

Although wild rabbits and their domesticated cousins may seldom drink if feeding on succulent plant material with a high water content, clean, fresh water must always be at hand for pet rabbits — in winter and summer. It is a myth that rabbits don't need water. Unlike humans, who perspire when the weather is too hot, rabbits regulate their body temperature through increased breathing and greater intake of fluids. For this reason, rabbits drink more water than usual on hot days.

Rabbits that are fed almost exclusively on dry commercial food, such as nursing does, need to have an abundant supply of water available at all times. Indeed, every pet rabbit should have free access to as much fresh clean

Obesity

Make sure that your pet rabbit gets lots of exercise; obesity in rabbits can lead to heart disease and other ailments.

water as it wants. Refill the water bottle every day with fresh water at room temperature and clean the water bottle thoroughly on a daily basis to prevent bacterial buildup.

Daily requirements

A rabbit eats approximately four per cent of its body weight in food each day, so an adult rabbit of, say, 4.5 kg/10 lb in weight would need around 75 g/2½ oz of concentrates and greens daily, plus about 100 g/3½ oz of good hay. The best hay to feed is young hay. High-quality young hay is fresh-smelling and slightly greenish in colour. Old hay has not only lost much of its nutritive value, but is also dusty. Hay dust can be quite irritable to a rabbit's sensitive nasal passages. Although hay is best provided free-choice, it is unwise to give unlimited quantities of concentrates. Rabbits easily put on a lot of excess fat and it can drastically shorten their lives.

Pregnant does are fed as above but the amounts must be increased gradually to twice the normal feed by the end of pregnancy. Lactating does need more again. Increase the amount to three times the normal feed by the end of lactation (six to eight weeks after giving birth).

Right: *Be careful which wild plants you let your rabbit eat.*

CHAPTER SIX

Wild plants as a supplementary food for rabbits

- [ ] Caraway
- [ ] Chickweed
- [ ] Cleaver (goose grass)
- [ ] Clover (**Note:** some clovers such as Ladino or Red Clover may cause infertility, and Sweet Clover can induce a bleeding disease.)
- [ ] Coltsfoot (fresh or dried)
- [ ] Comfrey (allow to wilt slightly before feeding)
- [ ] Corn Marigold
- [ ] Corn Spurrey
- [ ] Cow Parsnip
- [ ] Dandelion
- [ ] Dead-nettles
- [ ] Bitter Dock (only before flowering)
- [ ] Green Sorrel (very small quantities only)
- [ ] Ground Elder (only use before shoots appear)
- [ ] Hogweed
- [ ] Knapweed
- [ ] Knotgrass
- [ ] Knotted Persicaria
- [ ] Pale Smartweed
- [ ] Scented Mayweed
- [ ] Scentless Mayweed
- [ ] Mugwort or Bitterweed
- [ ] Common Plantain
- [ ] English Plantain
- [ ] Hoary Plantain
- [ ] Ragwort (Some people say it is safe for rabbits and that the animals relish it. I regard it as possibly causing liver disease under certain conditions. Avoid it.)
- [ ] Shepherd's Purse
- [ ] Silverweed
- [ ] Canada Thistle
- [ ] Marsh Thistle
- [ ] Sow Thistle
- [ ] Welted Thistle
- [ ] Tree and shrub foliage — acacia, alder, apple, ash, beech, maple, mountain ash, mulberry, raspberry, pear, poplar, and willow
- [ ] Yarrow (fresh or dried)

CAUTION

■ Leaves of ash, alder, elm, maple and willow should not be given to lactating does.
■ Do not give leaves from peach or plum trees – they can be poisonous.
■ Young leaves should always be selected.
■ Old beech and birch leaves are indigestible.
■ Avoid bark from the acacia — it can be poisonous — by using only the youngest twigs.
■ Never give evergreen leaves.
■ Twigs and shoots from most deciduous trees and bushes and fruit trees are fine and much relished by rabbits.

FRUITS, PLANTS AND NUTS

Fruits are good — in moderation. Wild plants, such as dandelion leaves, clover, coltsfoot, comfrey, cow parsnip, knapweed, shepherd's purse and chickweed, can also be offered, (see opposite for a comprehensive list with comments) but you should avoid areas, such as road verges, where pesticides may have been sprayed and always wash the food thoroughly before offering it to your rabbit. The following foods are all good for rabbits:

■ Acorns
■ Beechnuts
■ Black cherries
■ Hawthorn berries
■ Mountain ash berries
■ Privet berries (but not privet leaves)

Diet and tooth disease

Recently, some experts have suggested that because of the high incidence of tooth disease in pet rabbits, which can have extremely serious consequences, it would be best to omit concentrates from the diet altogether and feed the animals in a way more closely resembling that of their wild relatives where

Dangerous or risky plants for rabbits

This list is not exhaustive. If in doubt about any plant species, consult your vet. The effects on a rabbit of ingesting certain toxic plants can vary and may depend on a variety of factors: the amount eaten, the parts of the plant eaten, the condition or state of growth of the plant, the geographical location and the season of the year. Avoid the following plants:

- Anemone
- Autumn Crocus
- Azalea
- Bluebell
- Bryony
- Buttercup
- Celandine
- Dog's Mercury
- Figwort
- Fool's Parsley
- Foxglove
- Hemlock
- Henbane
- Holly Bindweed
- Laburnum
- Listeria
- Nightshades
- Poppy
- Purple Thorn Apple
- Rhododendron
- Spindleberry
- Toadflax
- Traveller's Joy (wild clematis)

Other plants that are dangerous at certain times or in certain conditions are:

- Bermuda or Couch Grass
- Bracken
- Caltrops or Puncture Vine
- Canary Grass (Australia, New Zealand and South Africa)
- Cherry Laurel
- Crotalaria, Ragwort
- Heliotrope
- Jimson Weed
- Lantana
- Loco Weed (USA)
- Lupin
- Paterson's Curse or Salvation Jane
- Rhododendron
- Sneezeweed (USA)
- Sweet Clover (particularly in USA)
- Tarweed
- White Clover
- White Snakeroot (USA)
- Yew

the teeth and jaws are well exercised constantly. They recommend nothing but free-choice hay and good fresh greens. However, it is known that tooth problems also have a genetic origin, so it is better to avoid the problem altogether and not buy a rabbit with bad teeth or consult your vet on how best to manage bad teeth.

Above: *Always hang a mineral lick in your rabbit's hutch or cage.*

Freshness

If you have only one or two rabbits, don't buy large quantities of food. It is better to buy small quantities of fresh materials frequently. Stored pellets and other forms of concentrates lose valuable vitamins and essential oils. When purchasing pellets, choose those that are the greenest and have the freshest smell, or look for a milling or expiry date on the pack.

Vitamins and minerals

A block of mineral lick should always be hung in the rabbit's quarters. Instinctively your pet will lick and nibble this to obtain any extra minerals it needs. It is also a wise precaution to supplement the water supply with vitamin drops.

Summary for feeding rabbits

The basic rules for feeding rabbits are as follows:

- Weigh concentrates and timothy hay.
- Supply small and varied quantities of greens and roots in the morning.
- Never neglect your pet's water supply.
- Make sure your pet gets lots of exercise; obesity in rabbits can lead to heart disease and other ailments.

CHAPTER SEVEN

Breeding rabbits

If you have both a buck and a doe and neither have been neutered, can you cope with the animals' proverbial fecundity? After all, it took only fifty years for rabbits to colonise Australia, and the most prolific breeds of rabbit can produce ninety to one hundred offspring per year!

Only if you can properly accommodate or find excellent guaranteed homes for the youngsters should you contemplate breeding from your rabbit(s). Otherwise, responsible ownership means having your rabbit or rabbits surgically castrated or spayed under general anaesthetic by a veterinary surgeon. Such neutering has other advantages. It removes the risk of uterine cancer (very common) in does and reduces the odour and spraying-tendency of bucks.

Did you know?

Rabbit's milk is the richest of all domestic animals with thirteen to fifteen per cent protein, twelve per cent fat and two per cent sugar (cow's milk contains three per cent protein, four per cent fat and five per cent sugar).

Fertilization

Does don't have an oestrus ('heat') cycle, unlike rodents, and can breed at any time of year although mating occurs more readily in spring and summer than in autumn and winter. Like the cat, the female rabbit does

not ovulate (shed fertile eggs from the ovary) spontaneously. Eggs are triggered instead by the act of mating. About twelve hours after mating some ovarian follicles rupture and release their eggs (ova) which pass into the Fallopian tubes and are fertilized there by the buck's spermatozoa.

Mating

If there is no oestrus cycle in rabbits, how can you tell when it is time to put a doe and buck together? Oestrus, the time when ripe eggs are present in the ovarian follicles, can sometimes be detected by inspecting the doe's vulva, which may enlarge and become purplish at this time. However, this sign does not invariably occur and, even when it does, some does won't accept the buck. The test is to see how the doe reacts when introduced to the buck — always take the doe to the buck, never the reverse, otherwise the female may attack the male, possibly injuring him. If you have more than one buck, you could try the doe with each of them.

Rabbits pick and choose their partners with as much care as we humans. Sometimes a doe will brusquely refuse one suitor only to fling herself with gay abandon at the next one. Obviously rabbit beauty truly lies in the eyes of the rabbit beholder.

Does become sexually mature at around six months of age but should not be mated before they are fully grown and developed: at least eight or, better still, ten months old. Bucks reach puberty at three to four months of age but only become sexually mature at around seven months.

Did you know?

The Surgeon-General's library in Washington DC possesses nine books and pamphlets devoted to the cases of women who were said to have given birth to rabbits in days gone by. One famous case was that of Mary Toft, an Englishwoman, who in 1726 claimed to have done so on several occasions. Many people throughout the country believed her until, after being closely watched, she confessed her claims were fraudulent.

Pregnancy

Pregnancy lasts about one month (twenty-eight to thirty-four days) and a doe may accept the buck at any time during pregnancy or false pregnancy. Rabbits can have several litters of two to eight young each year, although it is unwise to allow more than three litters per year for the sake of the health and long life of your pet doe. The average litter size is five youngsters but it can be as many as ten.

Did you know?

If a doe is mated while nursing a small litter she can become pregnant, whereas if she is nursing a larger litter (the minimum size varies with breed), the pregnancy will be curtailed after about five days.

Making a nest

During pregnancy the doe makes preparations for her babies by making a snug nest lined with soft fur plucked from her own coat. You should provide a shallow nesting box (5–7 cm/2–3 in deep) in the sleeping compartment of the hutch. Line the box with sawdust and hay or straw chopped into 10–15-cm/4–6-in lengths, and the doe should do the rest. If the doe does not adequately line her nest in the days leading up to her giving birth, add some sheep's wool or, if possible, some tufts of fur saved from a previous pregnancy. Once birth has occurred, however, you should refrain from touching the nest box unless absolutely essential.

Reabsorptiom

Sometimes the rabbit foetuses within the uterus (womb) will die during pregnancy and be aborted or, in early pregnancy, reabsorbed into the doe's body. This can be due to ill health, poor nutrition or a hereditary genetic factor. However, scientists believe that more than half the litters actually conceived are reabsorbed and this curious 'change of mind' by the doe's body is perfectly normal in most cases and may be Nature's last-minute attempt at population control.

CHAPTER SEVEN

False pregnancy

False or pseudo-pregnancy can also occur, as happens commonly in bitches and, far less frequently, in women. It may be caused by the death of foetuses (as already mentioned), by an infertile mating or by the presence of a lusty buck nearby.

An expert can detect pregnancy by gently feeling the doe's abdomen as early as nine days after mating. It's best if you don't try this yourself — your vet will do it.

During false pregnancy, which can last from fourteen to eighteen days, after which the doe is usually highly fertile, she exhibits the signs of true pregnancy, including nest-building and production of milk.

Did you know?

In normal births to does having a first litter, about one per cent of babies are stillborn. Overall, the ratio of male to female babies is exactly 50:50.

Diet in pregnancy

The food of a pregnant doe should be gradually increased so that by the time of birth, she is getting twice the normal ration. Greens and high-protein dry foods provide important nutrition at this time. Do not overfeed starchy and oily foods as excess fat in the mother and/or her babies can lead to difficulties when giving birth. Extra calcium and vitamin supplements, available from the pet store, should be provided on a regular basis.

Be careful when handling a pregnant doe. Do it only if absolutely necessary, and avoid all pressure on her abdomen.

Birth

The young rabbits are generally born at night. The event is rarely observed by the owner, the whole process taking ten to thirty minutes with seldom any complications demanding veterinary assistance. Very occasionally, there is a gap of several hours or even a day between the birth of one part of the litter and another. Each baby is born with its placenta (afterbirth) which the doe eats — a sensible provision by Nature that prevents fouling of the nest. After being licked clean by their mother, the babies (sometimes called kittens) promptly seek out the maternal teats and start nursing. Does have eight teats; consequently problems can arise with litters bigger than eight. If necessary, kittens (baby rabbits) can be fostered onto another doe if the latter's young are the same age and the switch is begun before the babies are three weeks old.

If a doe is mated while nursing a small litter, she can become pregnant, whereas if she is nursing a larger litter (the minimum size varies with breed), the pregnancy will be curtailed after about five days.

Many factors, including genetic ones, the age of the doe, the health, nutrition and number of previous litters, influence the litter size at birth. Does in tip-top condition and which are well

Below: *These rabbits are thirteen weeks old. From now on, young males should be housed singly to prevent fighting.*

CHAPTER SEVEN

nourished have bigger litters than ones that are in poorer shape and less well fed. The litter size generally increases over the first few litters, that is to say up to the age of about three years, and then gradually decreases thereafter.

The growing babies

At birth, young rabbits are helpless, with their eyes and ears closed and only a light down instead of fur. They are totally dependent on the warmth of their nest and the doe's body. You can make an initial inspection of the litter after they have all been delivered to see that all is well.

- Do not touch the kittens unless one is stranded outside the nest and heading for hypothermia.
- Remove any uneaten portions of placenta and, if there are more than eight in the litter, take away the extra ones in the shape of the smallest and weakest individuals and have them humanely euthanased by the vet. Do not drown them. Sometimes does kill their young if they have too little milk or for psychological reasons that are not understood.

Did you know?

Young rabbits double their birth weight within the first week of life. Human babies take six months to do the same.

By the end of the first week of life, the fur begins to grow. After ten days the eyes open; after twelve days the ears open; and by sixteen to eighteen days the kittens have begun to leave the nest and to nibble solid food. Then you can begin to handle the youngsters.

Caring for the kittens

To sex the kittens, look at their genital openings. Male rabbits have a round genital opening. Gentle pressure around it will extrude the penis. Female rabbits have a slit-like genital opening from which, of course, no penis can be extruded.

Kittens nurse for six to eight weeks and can then be considered weaned onto solid food, although some may continue to suckle the doe for a further week or two. At eight weeks, the young rabbits (except in the case of Angoras which should wait until twelve weeks of age) can be sent to good new homes.

It is possible but difficult to raise a baby rabbit on the bottle but cow's milk isn't rich enough to do the job: it doesn't contain nearly enough protein. So you will have to prepare a special formula milk. To make a suitable formula, extra protein in the form of 15 g/½ oz of calcium caseinate per 280 ml/10 fl oz of cow's milk must be added. This mixture is suitable until the kittens are seven days old after which the calcium caseinate must be increased to 17 g/⅗ oz per 280 ml/10 fl oz of milk. At fourteen days, the caseinate must be raised again to 20 g/¾ oz per 280 ml/10 fl oz of milk. The caseinate is mixed with the milk by whisking in a blender and will keep for several days in a refrigerator. Success has also been achieved in hand-rearing baby rabbits by using Cimicat milk subsititute for cats diluted one part to two-and-a-half parts with previous boiled water. Feeding should be given once every three hours, beginning at 6.00 a.m. and finishing at midnight. The milk mixture should be warmed to the kitten's body temperature before feeding by pipette or from a doll's feeding bottle complete with nipple.

Did you know?

'Chewer' a heavyweight (11 kg/25 lb) buck rabbit from Norfolk, fathered over 40,000 offspring between 1968 and 1973 before being retired.

After weaning, kittens are best kept in pairs or colonies although young males are best housed singly from three months onwards to prevent fighting.

Young rabbits should not be allowed to eat too much green food; it can lead to serious, possibly fatal, digestive trouble. Make sure they get plenty of hay and offer very small quantities of green food several times a day so that they are compelled to eat the hay in between.

CHAPTER EIGHT

Rabbit health

If a rabbit is off-colour or has an accident you need to know what to do — and do it quickly. This chapter acts as a guide for the observant, caring owner.

SIGNS OF ILLNESS

Rabbits are, in general, healthy, robust creatures who seldom pay visits to veterinarians, but occasionally they fall ill or develop pathological conditions which necessitate prompt treatment. What do you look out for? Listed below are some of the more common signs of illness.

Loss of weight

A rabbit that becomes thin, usually with a loss of condition indicated by a more 'staring', duller coat, may be suffering from one of a number of internal diseases or parasitism. In such cases do not waste your time trying out 'condition powders' or 'tonics' — consult your vet instead.

Weight loss can be caused by pseudotuberculosis, chronic infections, liver disease or infestations with tapeworms, fluke worms or, the commonest parasite of all, coccidia. Coccidia are protozoans, invisible to the naked eye, that can attack the liver or intestines. Diarrhoea may or may not be associated with an infestation. Your vet will examine the rabbit and take specimens

of droppings to look for worms, coccidia or other disease-producing microbes.

Treatment: Only after diagnosis can the correct treatment — vermifuges appropriate to the worm type, sulpha drugs for coccidia or antibiotics for bacterial infections — be decided upon.

Hair balls

Sometimes loss of weight accompanied by lack of appetite and perhaps diarrhoea is due to fur balls in the stomach. As in long-haired cats, excessive grooming and swallowing of hair gradually builds up a firm, sticky mass in the stomach.

Treatment: Unlike cats, rabbits cannot vomit, so the hair remains trapped in the stomach. This condition can usually be treated medically by your vet, but in some cases surgery (gastrotomy) under general anaesthesia is required.

Dental problems

Wild rabbits look after their teeth naturally. They spend four hours each day cropping grass and fibre-containing plants, consuming a diet that is both healthy and keeps the rabbit's mouth and its contents in great shape. Not for them the easy sometimes

Looking for signs of illness

You should check your rabbit over regularly to make sure that it is in good health. Some common signs of illness are listed below. If you discover any, take your pet to the vet so that it can be examined and a suitable treatment prescribed.

■ **Coat** — Is the coat 'staring' and duller than usual? This may indicate parasitism or internal disease.

■ **Ears** — Are there any scabs, scaling or inflammation? These may be telltale signs of ear mites.

■ **Eyes** — Is there any abnormal discharge or are they bloodshot? Wash with a warm saline solution and consult your vet.

■ **Hind legs and belly** — Are there any signs of infection on the belly or beneath the hind legs? This could be wet eczema.

■ **Lumps and bumps** — Can you feel any under the rabbit's skin? They may be abscesses so check with your vet.

■ **Nose** — Is there any nasal discharge? This may indicate respiratory infection. See your vet urgently.

■ **Skin** — Are there any scabs, ulcers or sores? These may be due to ringworm or mange.

■ **Tail area** — Is there any soiling of the fur under the tail? Are the rabbit's stools soft? These may indicate diarrhoea so check it out with your vet.

■ **Teeth** — Are they overgrown with plaque formation or cavities? If so, consult your vet.

■ **Weight** — Has your rabbit lost weight and got thinner? This may be a sign of chronic infection, parasite infestation or liver disease.

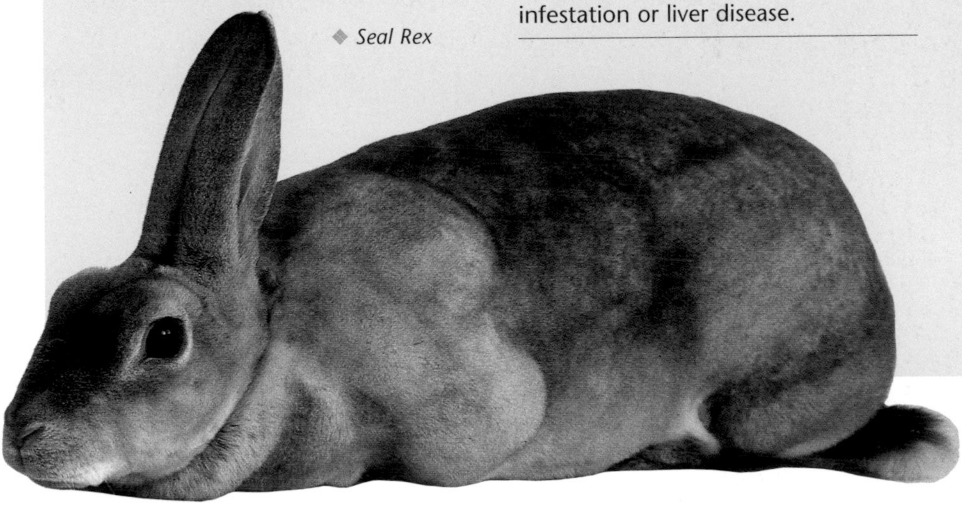

◆ *Seal Rex*

CHAPTER **EIGHT**

'spoiled' life of the pet bunny where, all too often, we find unwittingly poor husbandry practised by owners who overdo the commercial rabbit food and 'treats' that are rich in starch, low in roughage and which give the teeth little work to do.

The results are pet rabbits suffering from a range of common dental problems, including overgrown or weakened teeth, plaque formation and caries (cavities). These can subsequently lead to secondary, potentially serious disease.

How to avoid all this? Let your rabbit eat more like its wild cousins — concentrate on hay and green foods that need chewing. Your pet, too, should chew for at least four hours each day, and the dwarf breeds, whose teeth are disproportionately large, should be chomping away for about six hours.

Do not try clipping overgrown front teeth yourself — it can be very cruel, causing pain and even shattering of the teeth, which may spark off abscesses.

Investigation of mouth and tooth troubles in the rabbit's mouth is done by the vet looking in through an auroscope, the instrument normally used for inspecting ears, or by radiography. An increasing number of vets are now providing specialist dentistry services for rabbits, I am glad to see.

Treatment: Your vet will trim back any excess tooth growth with a dental bur and other instruments, where necessary under sedation or anaesthetic. Incidentally, rabbits going to the vet for a general anaesthetic for some reason should not be starved at all beforehand. This is because rabbits cannot vomit and also because post-operative recovery is quicker in rabbits fed right up to the time of surgery.

Constipation

True constipation is very rare in rabbits. Usually the absence of droppings is due to the animal not eating, perhaps because of a hairball or tooth problems. Gastro-intestinal stasis associated with bad feeding is, however, very common. Where the diet is low in fibre, there is insufficient water supply, or the animal is obese or inactive, the stomach may gradually lose its normal movement patterns. Then this gastric stasis leads to the accumulation of dehydrated food and fur balls in the stomach. The intestine can be similarly affected, in some cases concurrently. True gastro-intestinal obstruction where a ball of food and hair or some foreign body, perhaps a piece of plastic or rubber, blocks the valve between the stomach and duodenum or the junction between the small and large intestines, is less common.

Treatment: If no droppings have been passed by a rabbit in over twenty-four hours or if stool quantities gradually decrease, particularly when associated with loss of appetite and abdominal pain, ***contact your vet without delay.*** Do not waste time giving your rabbit laxatives.

Diarrhoea and enteritis

Enteritis (inflammation of the bowel) and diarrhoea can be due to many factors: diet, stress, bacterial infection, parasites, disease outside the gastro-intestinal tract and use of antibiotics.

Dietary causes

Perhaps the commonest cause is the overgrowth of abnormal bacterial flora in the bowel brought on by dietary indiscretion

resulting in toxins and gas production and, often, death.

Chronically soft stools which may have a strong odour and high mucus content are generally the result of diets that are low in fibre and/or too high in starch. Obesity and a sedentary life-style are often also present.

Treatment: Such cases respond to a diet of nothing but good meadow hay for two to three weeks followed by a gradual reintroduction of fresh greens, vegetables and fruit over a further month. It is best for such patients never to have concentrated foods or cereals ever again. Naturally they should be encouraged and enabled to exercise regularly.

Enterotoxaemia

The most dangerous form of enteritis commonly called enterotoxaemia, is caused by a rapidly multiplying bacterium called *Clostridium spiroforme*. This bug does its damage by producing a powerful poison or enterotoxin. The condition is characterized by profuse watery, sometimes bloody, diarrhoea and profound depression. Death ensues within one to two days. Enterotoxaemia is seen most often in newly-weaned young rabbits but can also occur after the use of certain antibiotics in rabbits of any age.

Antibiotics which should be avoided, if at all possible, for use in rabbits include: amoxycillin, ampicillin, cephalexin, clindamycin, erythromycin, lincomycin, penicillin and tylosin.

Treatment: Treatment of enterotoxaemia is difficult and the death rate is quite high.

Emergency treatment for diarrhoea

- Do not restrict liquid intake.
- As a first aid measure, substitute cold camomile tea for the drinking water.
- Keep the patient warm.
- Seek veterinary care quickly, as diarrhoea can often be an indication of serious life-threatening illness.
- Precise diagnosis usually involves sending samples of droppings to the laboratory and hospitalization of your pet.
- If your pet dies, remember that a postmortem examination by the vet will give valuable information, particularly where any other animals may be at risk.

Other bacteria and viruses

These can occasionally cause enteritis in rabbits.

- **Salmonella infection** from rodent-contaminated food or bedding or contact with animals carrying the bacteria (perhaps without symptoms) can occur. The only signs may be diarrhoea and dullness. It can result in death, particularly in young rabbits.

Treatment: Veterinary treatment involves the use of antibacterial drugs, usually after taking a stool sample for laboratory examination to determine the type of bug and its sensitivity to particular antibiotics.

- **Mucoid enteritis** is another, commoner, cause of diarrhoea. It usually combines diarrhoea with severe emaciation. The cause is

not well understood and may be due to a number of factors. It affects rabbits of all ages, ending fatally in most unweaned animals and occasionally in adults.

Treatment: There is no sure treatment for mucoid enteritis.

'Colds' and snuffles

A common ailment of rabbits carries the colloquial name 'snuffles' and, indeed, the animal looks rather as if it has a bothersome, snuffly, respiratory infection similar to a human 'cold'. The acute form shows a cloudy, white or yellowish nasal discharge together with fever. Death can follow quickly from pneumonia.

Milder forms exhibit sneezing and eye discharge and little else. The usual cause is a bacterium, Pasteurella multocida, a normally harmless resident of the rabbit's nose and throat which becomes a disease-producer when the animal's resistance is reduced, typically by stress.

Sometimes other bugs, such as *Staphylococcus,* are involved. In chronic cases, severe damage to the sinuses of the head can occur.

Treatment: This is by antibiotics of the tetracycline or quinolone families. Where there are eye symptoms, antibiotic and sometimes corticosteroid drops may be prescribed. Veterinary attention must be obtained early in all snuffles cases to prevent progression to pneumonia or intractable chronic sinusitis.

Taking your rabbit's temperature

You can take the temperature of your rabbit by inserting a stubby-ended electronic clinical thermometer made of plastic and metal — not glass — into the rectum. The normal temperature of a healthy rabbit is between 38.6°C/101.5°F and 40.4°C/104°F (much higher than in a human) with an average of 39.4°C/103°F. Do not use a glass thermometer as it may break inside if the rabbit struggles.

Skin troubles

A variety of skin ailments can affect the rabbit. You will detect them early if you handle and check over your pet regularly.

Skin disease

Broken fur, scurfy or scabby skin, ulcers, weeping sores and irritated areas need veterinary attention to ensure correct diagnosis and appropriate therapy. Fungi (ringworm), mange, various kinds of bacteria and pox virus can all attack the rabbit's coat. Samples need to be taken from affected areas for laboratory examination; this will involve the painless swabbing or scraping of the offending part. Ringworm usually comes from rats and mice, so make sure your hutches and runs are rodent proof.

Treatment: The disease is easily treated by putting anti-fungal drops in the food.

Lumps and bumps

If your rabbit develops one or more bumps under the skin, don't panic about myxomatosis (see page 123). Other things

are far more likely to be the cause of the rabbit's swellings.

Bumps can appear on the jaw, other parts of the head or virtually anywhere on the body. Usually they are not accompanied by loss of appetite, at least at first, and they may not seem particularly painful when touched.

The vast majority of these lumps are abscesses caused by various types of bacteria that arrive either through the bloodstream or gain entrance via a bite wound. A small minority are tumours and are operable if caught early.

Treatment: All bumps and lumps need veterinary attention. Abscesses may be lanced or completely excised under local or general anaesthetic and the veterinarian will also employ appropriate antibiotics.

Loss of hair and 'wet eczema'

Typically this affects the skin on the undersurface of the hind legs, particularly beneath the hocks, or under the belly of the rabbit. It is often caused by bad flooring (wire mesh) or lack of sufficient fresh litter on damp, dirty solid floors. Bacteria enter skin abrasions and nasty infections result. Rabbits housed or exercised outdoors are susceptible to fly strike and maggot infestation, which can be serious. Improved housing and management are the keys to a cure.

Treatment: This is by the use of antibiotic creams together with zinc ointment, human haemmorrhoidal cream or a baby anti-nappy rash preparation. The affected rabbit must be given dry soft bedding.

Quick guide to common rabbit parasites

Ear mange (mites)

■ *Symptoms:* Inflammation and scabbing inside the ears

■ *Look for:* Whitish or brown scaling inside ear, ear discharge

■ *See page:* 118

Mange on the body (mites)

■ *Symptoms:* Hair loss, scaliness and crustiness

■ *Look for:* Signs under the tail and on the dewlap

■ *See page:* 116

Fleas

■ *Symptoms:* Irritation and scratching

■ *Look for:* Flea droppings (look like black coal dust on skin)

■ *See page:* 116

Lice

■ *Symptoms:* Irritation and scratching

■ *Look for:* White eggs sticking to the hairs of the rabbit

■ *See page:* 117

Tapeworms, fluke worms and coccidia

■ *Symptoms:* Weight loss and diarrhoea. Parasites, however, can be present without causing symptoms.

■ *See page:* 105

❖ *Dalmation Rex Blue*

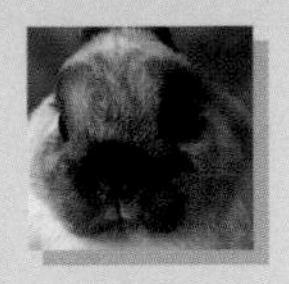

Rabbit syphilis

This disease is not infectious for humans or other animals and is common in domestic rabbits. It takes the form of weeping sores around the genital area, on the lips, eyelids and nose. Severe ulceration can obstruct the passage of urine and droppings, and if the germ spreads to internal organs, the rabbit may die.

Treatment: The bacterium that causes rabbit syphilis is similar to the one that causes syphilis in humans and it responds to injections of penicillin or other antisyphilitic drugs. Because of the risk of enterotoxaemia being triggered by penicillin, I prefer to treat this disease with oxytetracycline or enrofloxacin.

Mange

Mange mites very commonly infest the ears of rabbits (see page 118) but they can also affect the skin in other parts of the body, particularly under the tail and on the dewlap, causing hair loss, scaliness and crustiness.

Treatment: The condition is easily treated by modern antiparasitic preparations, such as Ivermectin, given by injection. Wherever skin disease is diagnosed, you must isolate the patient from other rabbits and clean and disinfect the hutch(es) and run thoroughly.

Fleas

Occasionally, rabbits, particularly those kept outdoors and in warm weather, can become infested with fleas. Several species of flea can feed on rabbits including dog and cat fleas. In the

United States, the Common Eastern rabbit flea may be encountered and curiously it prefers life in the fur of female rabbits. These parasites cause irritation and scratching. Usually there are telltale signs of flea droppings (looking like fine black coal dust) on the skin when the hair is parted.

Fleas can spread myxomatosis (see page 123), and thus control of fleas (and other insects such as mosquitos and house flies) is important, particularly if you live in the country and there is myxomatosis in the vicinity.

Treatment: This is with insecticidal sprays or powders of the type suitable for cats and containing permethrin but not fipronyl. Because the fleas' eggs fall off the rabbit's body and lie in the bedding and cracks in the hutch floor, sometimes for many months, before hatching, the animal's housing should be cleaned thoroughly and treated with a special aerosol that destroys flea larvae in the environment and is effective for several months. This is available from your vet.

Lice and ticks

Lice

Irritation and scratching can also be due to the presence of lice in the fur. Their eggs are white and, unlike those of fleas, are cemented to the rabbit's hairs by a natural adhesive. When grooming a rabbit with a coloured coat you will easily spot them.

Treatment: Lice are rapidly eradicated by applying special insecticidal powders obtained from your vet or pharmacist.

CHAPTER EIGHT

Ticks

Particularly if you live in the country, ticks may be found from time to time gorging themselves on your rabbit's blood, their heads fixed firmly in its skin.

Treatment: Never pull ticks off. Kill them by smearing them with a little vaseline or butter; this prevents them breathing so that, after a while, you can pick them off. If ticks are a recurrent problem ask your vet for a suitable insecticidal spray or powder.

Ears

Being so large, I suppose you could expect that rabbits' ears might attract a large amount of trouble. It's true — ear mange caused by mites living inside the ears is the commonest ailment of our rabbit friends. Luckily it is very rarely serious, easy to treat and even easier to prevent.

The mites don't suck blood but simply pierce and chew the skin lining the outer ear causing inflammation and a scabbing or scaling, sometimes whitish, sometimes brown, composed of dead skin cells, dead mites and mite droppings held together by serum oozing from the damaged ear.

Treatment: Your vet will gently clean out affected ears and prescribe anti-parasitic creams or drops. You should keep the ears in pristine condition by cleaning their inside surfaces once a month with cotton wool swabs dampened in warm olive oil.

Note: There can be as many as 10,000 mites in each ear. The irritation produced by these parasites can be so mild as to be almost unnoticeable or it may be severe, causing the animal to paw the offending organ and shake its head furiously.

Eyes

The most common eye troubles are runny, perhaps with a white or yellowish creamy discharge, and often bloodshot eyes on one or both sides. The cause may be a mild injury, a fly-borne infection or the presence of snuffles (see page 112).

Treatment: Wash the eye carefully with warm saline or human eye wash, available from a pharmacist, wiping away any crusting around the eyelids. If the condition persists for more than forty-eight hours or appears to be getting worse, consult your vet. Antibiotic or sulpha eye preparations may be indicated.

Nervous system

Paralysis

Loss of function, paralysis, of the hind parts can be due to violent struggling during handling or some other form of injury. It is a very serious condition needing immediate veterinary attention, which usually includes X-raying. Medical treatment is helpful in a minority of cases, but if there is not the first evidence of significant improvement within three weeks of the onset of paralysis, the outlook is bleak.

A specific type of paralysis with the unwieldy name of encephalitozoonosis is now considered to be fairly common in

domestic rabbits, particularly in North America. The cause, a protozoan that lives inside body cells can affect rodents, monkeys, cats, dogs and, importantly, human beings whose immune system is at a low ebb as in the case of AIDs patients.

The symptoms are paralysis of the rear end of the body, tremors, a tilted head (see Middle Ear Disease, below) urinary incontinence, stiffness, convulsions and eventually, after some weeks in most cases, death. Usually the disease spreads through the urine of an infected rabbit. At present there is no effective treatment for this serious complaint. Your vet can confirm its presence in an animal by a blood test.

The commonest reason for a rabbit tilting its head and, later, developing a tendency to move in circles but without any other symptoms is not the protozoan disease just mentioned, but rather Middle Ear Disease, an infection of the ear chamber just beyond the ear drum. This disease is often associated with a recent attack of snuffles, perhaps one as mild as merely a runny nose and watery eyes.

Treatment: A bacterium, commonly *Pasteurella*, is the usual cause and treatment is by a prolonged course of appropriate antibiotics. Chronic cases, particularly where the inner ear is also affected, can be very difficult to resolve. In a few instances, your vet may recommend surgery to drain the middle ear chamber.

Genito-urinary system

Troubles in the rabbit's waterworks department are rather common. Possible symptoms of abnormalities in the urinary system include wetness/skin scalding around the genital area beneath the tail, straining to pass water, thick creamy urine, or blood in the urine. It should be noted, however, that an orange or reddish urine can sometimes be due to digestion of some vegetable component of the diet, such as beetroot or other plants containing pigments. Your vet can quickly ascertain whether blood is present in the urine by means of a sample test.

Urinary ailments include kidney disease, cystitis and bladder stones or sludge. Rabbits differ from most domestic pets in the way in which they deal with calcium in their diet. Dogs, cats and budgerigars have mechanisms for absorbing just as much calcium as the body needs. Any excess in the grub is not taken in, or quickly excreted with the bile in the faeces.

Rabbits, on the other hand, absorb all the calcium they are fed and excrete the excess through the urine. Thus a very high calcium level in the diet can lead to lots of calcium in the urine. This calcium can then precipitate in the bladder or urethra, forming stones or sludge and perhaps causing a blockage. Rabbits given large amounts of concentrate pellets, cereals or bread, or with a restricted water supply and particularly those that are overweight, are most likely to be affected.

Treatment: By means, when appropriate, of urine tests, blood tests and radiography as well as hands-on clinical examination, your vet can determine the particular type of urinary disease. Depending on the diagnosis, antibiotics, catheterization to flush out the bladder or cystotomy (operating to open the bladder) will be indicated. Here, once again, we see the wisdom of making our pet rabbit's diet mainly one of hay, greens, fruit and non-starchy vegetables, with unlimited access to water.

The uterus (womb)

There are two main diseases of the doe's uterus: cancer and pyometra. Cancer, in the form of adenocarcinoma of the uterus, develops in at least fifty per cent of female rabbits (some experts say ninety-five!) by the time they reach five years of age. Pyometra, an infection of the uterus, is common in does over one year old. Both diseases may present vague symptoms at first. There may or may not be abdominal enlargement and general malaise, and there may or may not be discharge from the genital passage of white, yellow, pink or red-brown matter, sometimes smelling most unpleasantly.

Treatment: By drugs and/or surgery (hysterectomy) but, as ever, prevention is better than cure. Spaying does that are not required for breeding when they are six months old (at four months for dwarf breeds) solves the problem.

Mastitis

Inflammation of the doe's mammary glands is most often seen when her litter is weaned abruptly and/or early (rather than at eight weeks of age). The teats are swollen and inflamed and the condition can become very serious, even leading to death.

Treatment: Fomentations, using cotton wool dipped in warm water and massaging the teats with warm olive oil, done regularly throughout the day, are useful treatment aids, but antibiotics are generally indicated. I recommend a course of broad spectrum antibiotics given for seven to ten days.

OTHER SPECIFIC DISEASES

Tyzzer's Disease

This is an infection caused by a bacterium, *Clostridium piliforme*, which can attack many animal species including rabbits. In pet rabbits it can be present without producing symptoms, and its development into a full-blown, clinical illness may be triggered by stress, such as overcrowding, environmental or diet changes, transportation, weaning or the presence of other disease. Old age and antibiotic therapy may also play a part. The disease is transmitted by the ingestion of bacterial spores in the droppings of another infected animal.

The liver and intestines are the main areas attacked by the germ, and symptoms can range from poor appetite and soft droppings to profound lethargy, loss of appetite and watery diarrhoea.

Treatment: Tyzzer's Disease cases need prompt veterinary attention. Treatment can include fluid therapy, antibiotics and anti-inflammatory drugs but total success in eradicating the bug is difficult to achieve.

Myxomatosis

This is undoubtedly the most notorious rabbit disease. A viral infection, it was first described in 1893 in domestic rabbits in Uruguay. Apparently, the germ is widespread among wild South American rabbits that have built up a comparatively strong resistance to its attack. Attempts to control the rabbit population

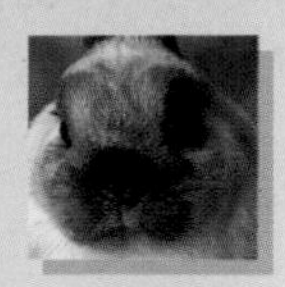

CHAPTER
EIGHT

Preventing myxomatosis

Domestic rabbits are not commonly at risk but if you live in the country and have wild rabbits entering your garden, you should take the following precautions:

- Protect the rabbit hutch from penetration by outsiders with wire mesh — five strands per centimetre/ten strands per inch.
- Using insecticides and restricting the use of runs when you hear of myxomatosis in the area.
- Best of all is a protective vaccine that is now available. Consult your vet.
- Where vaccination is not available, keeping your rabbit indoors to prevent exposure is advisable.

in Australia were relatively successfully by introducing the virus, although strains of rabbits resistant to the disease soon appeared.

In 1953, the virus was deliberately introduced into France; it quickly got out of control and swept through the largely non-resistant rabbit population of Europe, causing almost 100 per cent fatalities. It arrived in Britain in October 1953, striking first at colonies in Kent and Sussex. Wild rabbits are the natural reservoir host in North America. A highly virulent strain exists in California and Oregon and is spread by mosquitoes and other arthropod vectors.

Myxomatosis is spread by the bite of rabbit fleas in Europe and by mosquitoes in Australia, and also by direct and indirect contact. Among wild rabbits, it spreads most rapidly in the spring during their peak breeding season. The reason for this is the intriguing fact that rabbit fleas themselves breed only on pregnant rabbits.

Signs of myxomatosis

After an incubation period of two to eight days, the animal will show one or more of the following signs of Myxomatosis:

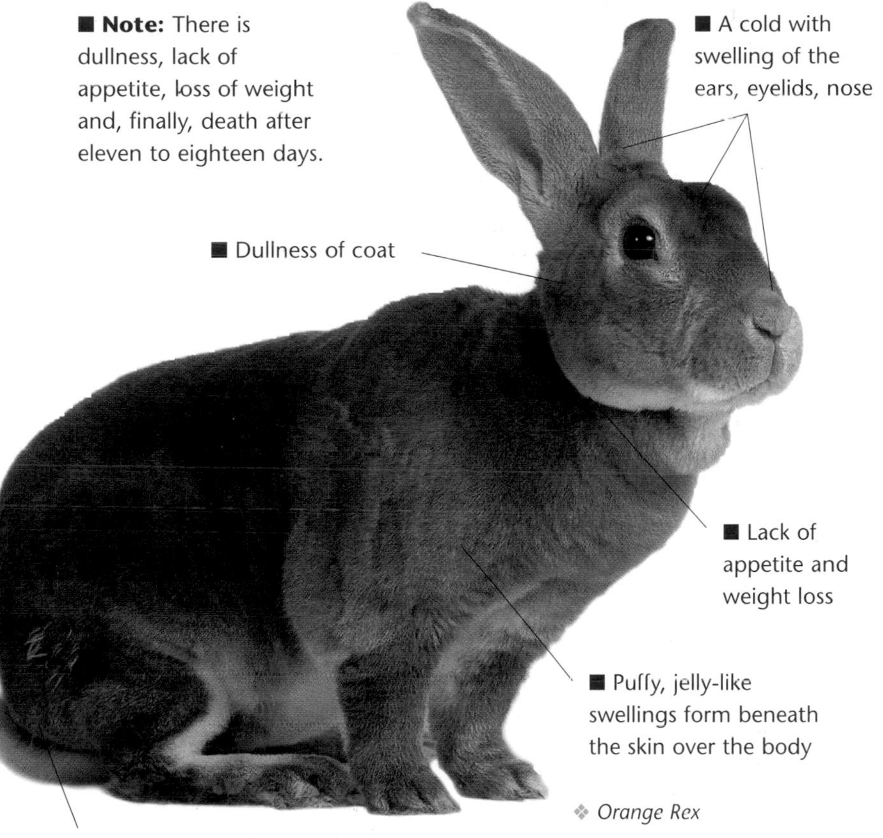

❖ *Orange Rex*

Treatment: This is very difficult, and antibiotics are of little value. Prevention can be achieved by vaccination and controlling fleas or other insect carriers.

CHAPTER
EIGHT

Viral haemorrhagic disease

This virus disease was first identified in China in 1984 and later reached Europe. By 1992, it had arrived in England. The only rabbit disease that must be notified to the authorities in the United Kingdom, it affects no other species except the rabbit, attacking mainly old bucks and does, but rarely their kittens under two months of age. It is highly contagious, spreading by airborne droplets, infected food, direct or indirect contact and, probably, being carried by birds.

Symptoms include sudden death, loss of appetite, fever, breathing difficulties, prostration, spasms, bloody nasal or eye discharge and groaning — a very nasty disease indeed. Although mildly affected animals can recover and become immune to further attacks, some die a few weeks after apparent recovery. Acutely affected rabbits usually die within one to three days of first becoming infected. Recovered immune rabbits can continue to spread the virus to other rabbits for at least one week.

Treatment: There is no treatment for this disease but an effective vaccine is available from your veterinary surgeon.

Useful contacts

United Kingdom
British Rabbit Council
Purfoy House
7 Kirkgate
Newark
Notts

The Rabbit Charity
PO Box 23698
London N8 0WS

FIRST AID

Small pets need expert attention in most cases when they fall ill or have an accident. Disease can proceed rapidly, sometimes to a fatal conclusion, and you should never waste time on patent remedies and experiments. In general, owners can do far less for the small pet, such as a rabbit, in trouble than for bigger animals, such as cats and dogs. Diagnosis and advice from your vet must always be sought without delay.

Fractures and sprains

Where it is suspected that fractures or sprains may have been caused by a fall or other trauma, do not attempt to splint the animal's legs with matchsticks or the like. Manipulating the delicate limbs can easily cause further serious damage to fine nerves and blood vessels.

Treatment: Pick the animal up by its scruff while lifting and supporting the hind quarters. Pain can be controlled in rabbits by the use of analgesic drugs. It is best to leave such medication to your vet. An injured rabbit may quickly enter a state of shock. Warmth is essential; wrap the animal in some soft material and take it to your vet without delay.

Small cuts and wounds

Treatment: Small cuts and wounds can be bathed gently in warm water and very weak antiseptic, and then dried. A tiny amount of antiseptic or antibiotic cream or ointment can then be applied to the cut or wound. However, powders are best avoided on hairy parts of the body as they tend to create matting.

Abscesses, 107, 114
American rabbit, 22
Angora rabbit, 29, 55, 61, 83, 84, 85
Argente rabbit, 22, 28
Behaviour, 41–43
Belgian Hare, 13, 26, 29
Beveren rabbit, 22
Birth, 100–102
Bladder stones, 121
Blanc de Bouscat, 74
Blanc de Hotot, 23
Body language, 42–43
Breeding, 97–103
British Giant, 23
Caecum, 53
Cages, 74–76
Calcium, 121
Californian rabbit, 23, 27, 66
Cancer, 122
Castration, 97
Cats, 58, 79, 80
Chin-scratching, 48
Chinchilla, 24
Choosing a rabbit, 60–61
Coccidia, 105, 106, 115
Colds, 112
Constipation, 109
Coughing, 62
Cross-breeding, 25
Cystitis, 121
Dangerous plants, 94
Dental problems, 53, 85, 94–95, 106–108
Diarrhoea, 63, 105, 107, 109–111
Digestive system, 53–54
Dogs, 58, 79, 80–81
Dutch rabbit, 30, 61, 66, 74
Dwarf rabbits, 24, 60, 74, 76, 81
Ear(s), 46, 47, 62, 107, 118–119
  Middle Ear Disease, 120
  mites, 107, 115, 118
Encephalitozoonosis, 119–120
English rabbit, 30, 37, 61
Enteritis, 109–110, 111
Enterotoxaemia, 110
Exercise, 90
  runs, 72
Eyes, 44–46, 62, 107, 119
False pregnancy, 100
Fancy breeds, 17, 21
Feeding rabbits, 86–95
Feet, 62
Fertilization, 97–98
First aid, 127
Fleas, 115, 116–117
Flemish Giant, 23, 26, 29, 31, 33, 51, 66, 74, 81
Florida White, 25
Fluke worms, 105, 115
Fractures, 127
French Lop, 16, 61
Fur, 55, 62, 63
  breeds, 17
Giant Papillon, 31, 74
Gnawing block, 70
Grooming, 84–85
Guinea-pigs, 58
Hair balls, 89, 106
Hair loss, 114
Handling, 83–84
Harlequin rabbit, 32, 37
Havana rabbit, 38, 74
Hay, 69, 71, 88, 89, 91
Heart disease, 90
Himalayan rabbit, 32, 55, 61
Holidays, 80
House rabbits, 57, 74–81
Housetraining, 60, 78–79
Hutch(es), 65–72
  minimum sizes, 66
Internal organs, 54
Kidney disease, 121
Lagomorphs, 14, 19
Leporaria, 15
Lice, 115, 117
Lilac rabbit, 27, 38, 61
Litter, 69, 71, 75
  boxes, 75, 78, 79
Liver disease, 105
Lops, 17, 34
Lotharinger, 33
Lumps, 113–114
Mange, 107, 113, 115, 116, 118
Mastitis, 122
Mating, 98
Middle Ear Disease, 120
Mineral licks, 95
Moulting, 55
Mucoid enteritis, 111–112
Myxomatosis, 13, 113, 117, 123–125
Nails, 62, 85–86
Nest making, 99
Netherlands Dwarf, 24, 35, 66
New Zealand rabbits, 12, 26, 61
Normal fur breeds, 20
Obesity, 88, 89, 90, 95, 110
Palomino rabbit, 36
Paralysis, 119–120
Parasites, 109, 115, 116–118
Perlfee, 26
Pneumonia, 112
Polish rabbit, 35, 36
Pregnancy, 99–102
  false, 100
  feeding in, 91, 100
Pseudotuberculosis, 105
Pyometra, 122
Reabsorption, 99
Refection, 54
Rex, 15, 17, 55, 74
  breeds, 21, 39
Rhinelander, 37
Ringworm, 107, 113
Sable, 27
Sallander, 27
Salmonella infection, 111
Satin breeds, 21, 38
Scent glands, 46, 48–49
Scruffing, 83
Sexing rabbits, 102
Silver rabbit, 13, 17, 37
Silver Grey rabbit, 12, 37
Skin, 107
  disease, 113–114
Smell, 46–49
Sneezing, 62, 112
Snuffles, 112, 119, 120
Spaying, 97
Sprains, 127
Sumatran hare, 9, 15
Sussex, 27
Swiss Fox, 28
Syphilis, 116
Tan rabbit, 37
Tapeworms, 105, 115
Taste, 49–50
Temperature, 68, 113
Territory marking, 46
Thrianta rabbit, 37
Thuringer, 27
Ticks, 118
Toys, 75
Transporting a rabbit, 69
Tyzzer's Disease, 123
Urinary disease, 120–121
Uterus, 122
Van Beverens rabbit, 61
Vienna Blue, 28, 66
Viral haemorrhagic disease, 126
Vitamins, 95
Vocal sounds, 51
Water, 88, 90–91, 95
  bottle, 70, 75
Weaning kittens, 103
Weight, 51, 107
  loss, 105–106
Wet eczema, 107, 114
Wild plants, 92
Wounds, 127